CONQUERING
FEAR

CONQUERING
FEAR

Karen Randau

Rapha
PUBLISHING

WORD PUBLISHING
Dallas · London · Vancouver · Melbourne

Conquering Fear
by Karen L. Randau

First Edition Copyright © 1991
Rapha Publishing/Word, Inc.
Houston and Dallas, TX

Names, locations, and other identifying characteristics in these stories have been changed. The events are real—they happen every day. It is the author's hope that the reader will gain insight and courage from the lives of these people.

Unless otherwise indicated, Scripture quotations noted are from The Holy Bible: New King James Version. Copyright © Thomas Nelson, Inc., Publishers 1979, 1980, 1982.

Printed in the United States of America
ISBN: 0-945276-22-2

To anxiety sufferers everywhere.

CONTENTS

ACKNOWLEDGMENTS

Thank you, Theresa Contreras, for your seemingly endless help in researching this book. Special thanks to my wonderful husband, Eric, for your love, patience, and understanding, and for reading and re-reading the manuscript to make sure I said what I thought I said.

FOREWORD

Until recent years, mental health professionals did not ascribe serious consideration to phobias. Studies in the past few years, however, have shown that inordinate fears are one of the most significant and debilitating mental health problems. Though fear itself is a normal healthy reaction which helps us respond accurately to threatening realities, phobias thrust our feelings and responses far beyond healthy responses. Indeed, these exaggerated fears—of heights, snakes, speaking in public, thunder, darkness, driving on highways, and virtually every aspect of human experience—are often focused on fear itself, that is the fear of becoming so afraid that we lose control and act in an embarrassing or destructive way.

Karen's research and writing provides not only truth, but genuine insight. She helps people understand why they feel and act as they do. Those who read her work identify strongly with her: "That's me! I feel that way, too!" "I didn't know anybody else but me ever felt that way!" "I've been hiding all my life, hoping no one would realize what's inside, but Karen understands me!"

This book explores the initially obscure causes of these fears and dispels the fog so that past wounds, broken relationships, and crushed dreams are clearly exposed. Then the process of hope, healing, and grief can take place.

A central theme in this book is the comfort and strength which God brings to those who are afraid. When the angel said to Mary, "Fear not!" or when Jesus spoke to the disciples, "Do not be afraid," they recognized that these were people who were afraid—terribly afraid!—but the words of grace and the presence of the Lord brought strength and courage.

As you read this book, take time to reflect and be honest with the Lord and with at least one other person about your fears and the causes of those fears. If possible, find a small group so that you can learn from one another and comfort each other as you probe the causes of your fears. The love of the group will also enable you to experience true healing as you focus on the Lord's patience, kindness, and strength.

I trust that Karen's vivid explanations will help you tremendously in your process of conquering fear.

Robert S. McGee
President, Rapha

INTRODUCTION

Research by the National Mental Health Institute shows that anxiety disorders affect 20 to 30 million people in the United States—10 percent of the population. Anxiety is the number one mental-health problem for women and second only to alcoholism/drug abuse among men.

Anxiety wraps itself tightly around your chest until it feels as if you will suffocate. People who suffer from anxiety attacks frequently attempt to hide the problem, rendering themselves isolated, lonely, and convinced that they are going crazy.

This book is intended to help you untangle the frightening mystery about anxiety. It will help you understand anxiety, loosen its grip, and put a breath of fresh air back into your life. You will also learn the skills necessary to overcome anxiety and discover some steps you can take to begin developing these skills. Recovery from anxiety will involve physical, psychological, and spiritual elements. This book covers all three areas.

A book is not a recovery program. But this book *can* give you ideas about how you can launch yourself into recovery.

1

What is Anxiety?

When I met Vicky, I did not understand what made her tick. As her coworker, I usually could tell what our day would be like by the expression in Vicky's eyes. Though I did not comprehend the significance at the time, her beautiful, huge eyes either gleamed with a spark of youthful cheer or appeared dark and fearful.

I once asked her, "What are you afraid of?"

"Nothing," she responded indignantly. The rest of the day, Vicky acted half her age. Though she tried to assume a happy demeanor, her dark, wide eyes provided an alarming signal. Something about her seemed familiar, but that "something" continued to allude me.

Days later, Vicky flippantly related a childhood memory of a time when the house was dark and a violent midwestern thunderstorm tore through her emotional fabric. She had hidden in an upstairs closet, rocking herself back and forth for comfort while she tearfully waited for one of her parents to come home.

As she told the story, her eyes filled with the darkness that I had learned to recognize as "a bad day." I watched her fidget during the remainder of the workday. She seemed to have problems breathing at times. With sweat on her brow, she complained of being cold. She appeared to distrust everything and everyone.

As we got into our cars to leave the office, I said, "Drive carefully, Vicky."

"Traffic terrifies me," she said, and she laughed nervously as she gracefully slipped into her flashy sports car. "I sometimes have to pull over a few minutes to find my composure."

At that moment I was struck by a blinding glimpse of the obvious. I froze with one leg in my car and the other supporting my weight on the ground. My chin dropped as I realized, *Vicky has anxiety attacks!* And the "something" that seemed familiar about her behavior was suddenly clear. *I had been seeing myself in her.*

Traffic was just one of the many things that used to frighten me. My life was dictated by fear. I agonized over everything, and if I did not have anything to worry about, I invented something. I even put myself into situations that caused crises—just to experience a "normal" feeling of excitement. Unfortunately, the excitement often got out of control, and then I became afraid.

From the time I was very young, I often excused myself from gatherings to slip into the restroom while a wave of nervous fear electrified my body. I had never outgrown it. The practice culminated my first day at a new job immediately after college. I stood in the corner of the restroom with my hot face pressed firmly against the cool tile. Desperately trying to regain a sense of reality, I felt myself slipping to the floor. As I lost consciousness, my head hit the hard tile.

I had put myself through such an emotional wrestling match that my body would no longer support me. When I began to come to, I felt sweat dripping down the side of my face and body. Goosebumps formed on my arms.

A woman startled me when she entered the restroom. "Are you OK?" she asked with concern.

I didn't want to appear weak, so I lied. "Oh, yes," I said as brightly as I could. "I got hot and thought the tile would help me cool off."

The woman rolled her eyes and went about her business. But she made it a point to avoid me during the three years we worked together.

I had finally worked through my anxiety attacks. I found a capable therapist and read dozens of self-help books. Eventually God led me out of the anxiety that had caused most everything in life to incapacitate me. And as I sat in my car and watched Vicky drive away, I wanted to help her.

"But how?" I asked God. "I'm not a therapist."

The spirit of God spoke to my heart, "No, my child, but you've been there."

Hmmm. I started my car to drive home. *I thought I was just depressed.*

The following day I began researching the causes of (and solutions for) anxiety. I wanted to help Vicky, but I also ended up understanding myself much better. I began to realize that I caused my own depression by allowing

anxiety to seize control of my life. Understanding myself
eased the burden I used to place on my emotions. As I
learned more about my anxiety, I also discovered how it
was connected to other feelings I had, including
depression, panic, and fear.

Smoke Signals

Fear is a healthy reaction to physical or spiritual
harm. It is a smoke signal that alerts us to danger and the
need for action. It sometimes triggers an adrenalin rush,
but it may also be accompanied by unhealthy doses of
anxiety.

One rainy night, a car pulled across the road in front
of me. Fear gripped my body. I had no choice but to hit
the brakes and skid sideways.

I collided with an oncoming car as my seat belt
tightened and my arms, legs, and head thrashed
uncontrollably. I wasn't hurt, but I was stunned and unable
to move for several seconds. Someone ran to my car and
opened the door.

"Are you all right?" asked a strange man.

"I think so," I answered, unfastening the seat belt.

I began to shake and then to cry. The sudden burst
of emotion had zapped my energy and ability to think. *I
never want to drive a car again—or ride in one for that
matter*, I told myself. But the intensity of my feelings
soon dissipated and before long I was back driving the
same winding road to and from work each day.

Yet for years following the accident, driving in heavy
traffic would cause every muscle in my body to tighten
as I white-knuckled the steering wheel. My healthy fear

in response to real danger turned into anxiety over a danger that may or may not exist. Though I was still able to drive, I was extremely uncomfortable about it. If I could have avoided it, I would have.

Caught Up in the "What Ifs"

While fear focuses on an immediately impending danger (such as a car wreck about to happen), anxiety is a constant level of internal tension over something that may or may not occur in the future.

According to Edmund J. Bourne, Ph.D., anxiety is "vague, distant, or even unrecognized danger...about losing control...about something bad happening" (*The Anxiety and Phobia Workbook*, New Harbinger Publications). Occasionally anxiety may be warranted. It may be a red flag that tells you something is wrong. In my book *Life Doesn't Have to Hurt* (Thomas Nelson), I wrote about Susan, who experienced a repeated tugging in her stomach (a sign of anxiety) each time she saw her husband and daughter together. After discovering that her husband was sexually molesting her daughter, she removed him from their home.

Susan's feeling of anxiety was related to a specific problem for which she had good reason to be concerned. We also tend to worry about other genuine concerns such as bills, family issues, jobs, and security. Yet Jesus clearly tells us not to worry about such things (Matthew 6:25–34). So is anxiety ever truly *healthy*?

The key is in how we respond to those first pangs of anxiety. If, after we begin to experience anxiety, we immediately focus our attention on God rather than our own inability to control circumstances or others' actions, our response is indeed healthy. Later chapters will help you learn to focus your attention on God and respond in a healthy manner.

Anxiety can also produce unhealthy responses that have little to do with the present and often linger for years. Some people let anxiety take over and begin to shirk responsibility. The roots of this type of anxiety are firmly implanted in past events. Scenes of the past start playing in their heads, and they superimpose previous pain over what *might* happen in the future. You may not know exactly what you're afraid of, or even that something bad is sure to happen, but you choose to respond to fear anyway.

Bourne says that anxiety affects your body ("rapid heartbeat, muscle tension, queasiness, dry mouth, or sweating"), behavior ("your ability to act, express yourself, or deal with certain everyday situations"), and psychological health ("detached from yourself...fearful of dying or going crazy").

Ken provides a good example. He played the piano skillfully—when he was alone or thought no one was listening. He found a particularly beautiful piece that he wanted to play in church, but the idea of performing in public gripped his head like a tight vice. Ken thought, *The solution is to spend months practicing until I can play the song in my sleep.* So he practiced until he could play the song flawlessly.

On the day of his performance, Ken walked to the piano thinking uncomfortably, *Dozens of eyes are staring at me.* An old tape started playing in his head as he recalled an embarrassing performance in the sixth grade. He was to play a solo in front of the whole school—with no music in front of him. Perhaps a little overconfident, he had not practiced enough. He forgot everything but three measures of the tune, which he repeated for two long, humiliating minutes. And for the next 15 years, he had carefully avoided all performances.

In front of the church congregation, Ken pushed the memory aside. But the damage to his self-confidence was already significant. Sitting at the beautiful piano, Ken looked at the keyboard. *Where do my hands go?* he thought in a foggy haze.

Don't panic, he warned himself. *I have practiced this song to perfection.* He placed his hands where he thought they might belong and started playing. The sound was horrible! He started over, and again he failed.

He stood up, looked at the pastor and said with shame, "I'm so nervous I can't play this song." His face burned in embarrassment. His stomach churned. *I'm losing my mind*, he thought in horror.

"It's OK, Ken," said the understanding young pastor. "Just calm down. You'll do fine."

"We want you to play," said a soft voice in the first row. The voice belonged to Ken's three-year-old daughter, Amy. He did not want to disappoint her, so he sat down and took a deep breath. The pastor bowed his head in prayer.

Think only of Amy, Ken ordered himself. Even though his hands continued to shake and sweat dripped from his

forehead, his performance was flawless. When he finished
playing, he returned to his chair without allowing his
eyes to meet anyone else's.

You miserable failure, he thought repeatedly
throughout the service. He was unable to concentrate on
the pastor's message. He experienced feelings of
depression for several weeks as a result of his perceived
failure.

Like many anxiety sufferers, Ken expected to fail
because he had failed in the past. He superimposed the
humiliation of a sixth-grade failure with an upcoming
event as an adult, causing himself to perform below his
ability.

Bourne defines four types of anxiety:

- *Free-floating Anxiety*—Sudden uneasiness not
  connected to a specific event and usually subsiding
  relatively quickly
- *Situational Anxiety*—Gradually heightening
  uneasiness connected to situations such as driving,
  seeing a doctor, or confronting someone
- *Phobia*—Fear that causes consistent avoidance of
  specific situations
- *Anticipatory Anxiety*—Intense worry about
  something that might happen during one of your
  phobic situations.

It is normal for people to experience any of these
forms of anxiety from time to time. But problems arise
when any type of anxiety escalates into an "anxiety

disorder." At this point the emotion becomes extremely intense (as in recurring bouts of panic), lasts months beyond the end of the stressful event, or interferes with normal functioning in the person's life. (Treatment methods for anxiety disorders will be discussed in later chapters.)

Because all types of anxiety produce a feeling of being out of control, any of them can easily accelerate into panic.

Get Me Out of Here—Now!

Panic is the unleashing of fear and anxiety. Symptoms include shaking, a racing heart, sweaty palms, ringing ears, dizziness, nausea, a feeling of losing sanity, chills, heat waves, choking, and intense loneliness. More than three panic attacks a month indicate what psychiatrists call a "panic disorder" which requires professional treatment.

In reference to panic, Bourne says that "the causes...involve a combination of heredity, chemical imbalances...and stress." Treatment methods are presented in later chapters and the Appendix.

My anxiety-prone coworker, Vicky, has occasional panic attacks. In fact, she had one the day I discovered she suffered from anxiety. She went to the airport to pick up a friend. Driving through heavy traffic caused Vicky to feel increasingly uncomfortable. She soon took a tranquilizer to maintain control.

Her mind raced. Her hands, cold and wet in spite of the dry, summer heat, slid on the steering wheel. Her breathing became quick and labored. A frightening "unreal" feeling rushed upon her. She rubbed her legs fiercely, hoping that contact with her own body would return her to reality.

Inside the terminal, sights and sounds crashed through Vicky's weakening composure. The walls seemed to be suffocating her. She stopped in front of the incoming flight monitor, desperately attempting to calm her frazzled nerves. She thought, *I have to act naturally, or the people around me will know I'm crazy.*

According to the flight schedule, she was supposed to find Gate 33. She blinked in disbelief and turned to look down the long, crowded hall leading to the gates. Gate 33 was beyond her field of vision.

She took a deep breath and started walking toward the hall, but she stopped abruptly. Turning away, she thought, *I can't go down there.* She ran to the baggage claim area instead, hoping to find fewer people and less commotion. *My friend can look for me here,* she rationalized.

Within moments, a tidal wave of people poured into Vicky's baggage-area refuge. A buzzer sounded, further confusing her hazy state of mind. A red light flashed atop a baggage carousel, which had begun to move. People crowded toward the carousel; a man inadvertently bumped into Vicky's shoulder.

The noise seemed deafening. Vicky fought her panic attack with all the mental strength she could find. "No," she said, thinking, *If I let these feelings get away from me, I'll go crazy. I'll end up locked in some institution for the rest of my life.* "No," she repeated. The more she fought the panic, the worse it seemed to get.

I'm going to faint, she thought in desperation. She leaned against the wall, holding her hand to her chest as she gasped for air. *I can't live like this anymore,* she thought as tears escaped from her huge brown eyes. She leaned against the wall until her tranquilizer took effect and she began to calm down.

When Vicky told me of this event the following day, I began my investigation into the nature of anxiety.

What Causes Anxiety?

Anxiety is a symptom of emotional overload when you no longer recognize and deal with your own feelings. You learn to deny them by either concealing them or disguising them as something else. And until your emotions are exposed and put into perspective, they will continue to haunt you.

My car wreck caused me to fear traffic; my anxiety about starting a new job prompted me to faint and then lie about it. Ken allowed a past failure to prevent him from sharing his talent, and it nearly destroyed a performance for which he was completely prepared. Vicky's anxiety became so out of control that she took tranquilizers to ward off frequent panic attacks that were brought on by everyday living.

What forms does your anxiety take? Bourne names several different kinds of anxiety disorders, listed on the following page.

- *Agoraphobia*—Fear of being in open spaces, having panic attacks, or being in a place where escape would be difficult
- *Social Phobias*—Fear of being embarrassed
- *Simple Phobia*—Fear of a specific object or situation
- *Generalized Anxiety Disorder*—Persistent worry that continues at least six months
- *Obsessive-compulsive Disorder*—Recurring, yet senseless ideas, thoughts, images, or impulses (obsessions) and the behaviors (compulsions) that are intended to alleviate the anxiety produced by the obsessions.

The exercises in this book are designed to help you recognize the roots of your anxiety and deal with the emotions that cause it.

You are likely to discover—sometimes surprisingly—that you are conditioned to live in fear and discontent, and rarely allow yourself to feel or express hurt and anger. You may have been taught that your feelings are wrong or insignificant. Possibly you have experienced so many disappointments that you have given up on yourself.

Overcoming Anxiety

You choose your response to anxiety. You may allow your emotions to become so out of control that they completely ransack your life. Interestingly, choosing to live with anxiety focuses attention on yourself even while it shatters your self-confidence. People caught in anxiety may find it difficult to concentrate, make wise decisions, or feel successful. Possibly they have a hard time getting along with others, or they often feel unhappy, tired, or ill. Four steps are necessary to overcoming anxiety: uncovering negative emotions, learning to forgive, being honest with oneself and others, and living a balanced lifestyle. The intent of this book is to help you learn these skills through a journey of self-discovery.

Be honest as you examine yourself in the "Looking Inside" section at the end of each chapter. If you suffer anxiety, you have years of muffled emotions and thoughts that you must uncover. Only then will you discover the root causes of your anxiety...and be able to deal with them.

The first step in overcoming anxiety is understanding it. Realize that you are not alone. Thousands of people just like you struggle to slay the dragons that lurk behind their every activity while they wonder what is wrong, afraid someone will find out.

Keep in mind that you are precious to God (1 Peter 2:4). Everything you feel and everything you think is important to Him. As one of His treasured children, He does not want you to suffer from out-of-control emotions.

The process of discovering yourself and confronting your feelings will hurt at times. You may uncover suppressed memories that you are unable to deal with alone. Seek professional help if you need it. But by all means, stay with it.

Looking Inside: Anxiety Inventory

1. Listed below are some characteristics common to many anxiety sufferers. Check the traits that describe you. Use the space on the next page to further personalize your list.

❑ I strive to impress others.

❑ I believe I must live up to the expectations of others.

❑ I am often unable to cope with daily activities of life.

❑ I accept guilt for events beyond my control.

❑ Feelings of inadequacy dominate me.

❑ My stomach is often upset or acidic.

❑ A tight band frequently seems to encircle my head.

❑ I am a perfectionist.

❑ I am often afraid or tearful, even when I don't know why.

❑ I sometimes feel paranoid.

❑ I have bouts of diarrhea or constipation.

❑ I use prescription or illicit drugs to settle my nerves.

❑ I use alcohol to calm my nerves.

❑ I am quick to anger.

❑ I suffer from insomnia, or I sleep too much.

❑ I have a tendency to sabotage personal and professional relationships.

❑ I refrain from displays of emotion, fearful that I might lose control or go crazy.

❑ I am ashamed to let others see below the surface of my personality.

❑ I believe that my problems are too big for God to solve.

❑ I believe I am unworthy of God's love and forgiveness.

❑ I feel unworthy of love.

❑ I often feel that I am stuck in quicksand, and the more I try to get out, the deeper I sink.

❑ I panic easily.

❑ I sometimes feel that I'm walking around in a dream.

Other:

2. List below the names and/or characteristics of the *people* who cause you to feel uneasy (i.e., men, policemen, powerful people, your spouse, your parents, etc.).

3. List below the *places* in which you remember having experienced anxiety attacks (i.e., the car, church, school, strangers' homes, in crowds, etc.).

4. List below the *things* or types of *events* that cause you anxiety (i.e., being alone, airplanes, fear of dying, etc.).

5. When do you *most often* feel anxiety?

6. Under what kinds of circumstances does anxiety *most often* attack you (i.e., when far from home, getting too far away from a safe person, etc.)?

7. How do you react to your anxiety (i.e., run, take drugs or drink alcohol, tell jokes, hide, get angry, etc.)?

8. What are the physical ramifications of your anxiety (i.e., ulcers, migraines, sleeplessness, hives, etc.)?

9. Read Isaiah 41:10. What does this verse say to you about your anxiety?

10. Read 1 John 4:18. What does this verse tell you about your worthiness to be forgiven of your sins? About God's grace and ability to deliver you from your anxiety attacks?

2
Who Is Likely to be Anxious?

Everyone is likely to experience anxiety from time to time. We are anxious when bills are due, when loved ones are sick, or when we are experiencing adversity. We are anxious to make a good first impression during a job interview or when meeting new people.

But why are some people more likely to be dominated by the emotions caused by anxiety?

In their book *Worry Free Living* (Thomas Nelson), authors Frank Minirth, Paul Meier, and Don Hawkins submit that "the more insecure we are, the more we strive for attention, fame, and success." It stands to reason that the more insecure you feel and the harder you try to impress others, the more likely you are to suffer from anxiety.

If that is true, why are some people more insecure than others? What causes these people to lose jurisdiction over their confidence and emotions?

As Edmund Bourne suggests, both "nature and nurture" can contribute to anxiety. My research indicates the "nature and nurture equation" consists of heredity, birth order, temperament type, and childhood memories.

Anxiety Genes?

According to Bourne, some people have a genetic predisposition for certain types of anxiety disorders: ". . . it is estimated that 15 to 25 percent of children growing up with at least one agoraphobic parent become agoraphobic themselves, while the rate of agoraphobia in the general population is only 5 percent." However, how much of this predisposition is inherited and how much is learned?

More convincing is Bourne's suggestion that if one identical twin suffers from some form of anxiety, "the probability of the other identical twin having an anxiety disorder ranges from 31 to 88 percent, depending on the study you're looking at."

Whether inherited or learned or both, mental health disorders are overcome by employing a balance of recovery methods. Some effective methods will be discussed in later chapters.

The Birth Order Puzzle

In *The Birth Order Book* (Thomas Nelson), Kevin Leman contends that there are four basic birth order categories: only child, first born, middle child, and last born (or baby).

A lot is expected of the first child, whose novice parents have no choice but "parental experimentation."

These children are often over-parented, ending up as adult perfectionists. Though proud parents usually give these first children plenty of praise for a job well-done, such comments can be interpreted as conditional, "we will love you *if*" statements. First-born children often take life seriously and seek constant approval.

Very similar to the first-born child is the only child. People in this category are lonely children, growing up with few friends or playmates. Mom and Dad are usually their closest friends. Consequently, these children may have a hard time getting along with peers. They prefer to be around either much older or much younger people. Children with siblings that are not close to their own age can also follow this pattern. Both first-born and only children tend to feel a lot of stress in their lives, making them good candidates for anxiety.

The personality of middle children is less predictable, depending upon the personalities of older and younger siblings. If the older sibling is "perfect," the middle child will try to carve out a separate (and often opposite) identity. Middle children may feel squeezed between their siblings, wondering if and where they fit in. These are compromising people and very concerned about being treated justly.

The last-born or baby of the family is great at getting attention. These children want—and often get—a majority of the attention in the house. Because parents and siblings suggest that they are "too little" to accomplish certain tasks, last-born children may tend to feel that they are unable to achieve.

A thorough study of birth order will be much more complex than what is presented here. But it is important to remember that birth order affects the way you perceive your position in life.

Temperament: The Unique You

A person's temperament is another factor to consider in our look at anxiety-prone people. Your temperament type adds dimension to your emotional reaction to life. The idea that temperament impacts behavior is not new. Early philosophers theorized about it. Thousands of people throughout history have further shaped the concept.

Many experts describe a "Type A" personality as the most likely to be troubled by anxiety. These are the hard workers who pay extreme attention to every detail, whether in their work, at home, or in personal appearance. They drive themselves to succeed in all they do and have little patience for people who do not share their passion for hard work. They often hold responsible leadership positions.

But what if you are an anxiety sufferer and not in the "Type A" group? Does this mean you are abnormal? I used to wonder about that myself because I am not a "pure" Type A. Then I came across an explanation of temperament types that gave me more insight into myself.

At a social gathering I heard someone say, "I'm a sanguine." I wondered at the time if this was some new kind of astrological terminology and dismissed the statement. But later I read Beverly LaHaye's book, *The*

Spirit-Controlled Woman (Harvest House), where she describes four basic temperament types: melancholic, phlegmatic, choleric, and sanguine.

I discovered that a melancholic person has a naturally gloomy outlook on life, constantly scrutinizing himself or herself. Such people are likely to be gifted, introverted, or even genius-prone, yet good candidates for anxiety! Their occupations are often creative or detail oriented.

Phlegmatics are introverted and calm. They seem to be easy-going with well-balanced temperaments, though they can be stubborn and indecisive. Because phlegmatics quickly acquiesce to their fate in life, they are less likely to suffer from anxiety. Likely members include homemakers, bookkeepers, teachers, administrators, and sports spectators.

Cholerics are active people who appear to have an endless supply of energy. These are strong, confident leaders who optimistically and fearlessly make major decisions. Cholerics tend to be rather selfish when it comes to considering plans, projects, and others' opinions. This temperament type is not naturally inclined toward anxiety. But coupled with other conditions—such as domineering and demanding parents—unhappy cholerics could become angry, insensitive people. They tend to hold very responsible jobs.

Sanguines are super-extroverts who tend to be the warm and lively lives of the party. Their occupations and hobbies indicate a need for attention: actors, speakers, athletes, salespersons, and so forth. They strive for approval and work hard to maintain it. A sanguine is an anxiety attack waiting to happen.

I have heard other people say that meloncholics have a compliant or analytical temperament, phlegmatics have a steady or amiable temperament, sanguines have an influencing or expressive temperament, and cholerics have a dominant or driven temperament.

In her book, *Personality Plus* (Fleming H. Revell), Florence Littauer offers a quiz to help decide which temperament describes you and how it affects your personality.

Most of us relate to a little of each temperament type. The important question to ask is which traits are dominant in regard to your emotional life. You can learn to capitalize on the positive traits of the temperament and alter the impact of the negative aspects.

As was true with birth order, an unhappy childhood tends to emphasize the negative traits of each temperament over the positive ones. (This is the "nurture" part of the nature and nurture equation.)

Childhood Memories: A Portrait of What's Inside You

Childhood memories reveal the breeding ground where your birth order and temperament type meld to form the adult you become. Your first memories provide an interesting filter for how you think, view life, form relationships, deal with emotions, and shape your self-image.

In their book *Unlocking the Secrets of Your Childhood Memories* (Thomas Nelson), Kevin Leman and

Randy Carlson suggest that out of the millions of memories adults accumulate over a lifetime, they recall "only those events from early childhood that are consistent with their present view of themselves and the world around them."

One of my first memories was romping in the yard outside my house with my older sister. She and I were inseparable; we were best pals. We laughed and ran, squealing with delight as only little girls (ages two and four) could. My hair bounced as I chased my sister and then she chased me. I wore only underwear, but I was in my own backyard, so I felt safe, free, and happy.

My bare feet seemed to glide through the grass and a wet spot where soft, slippery mud oozed through my toes. It was wonderful!

Suddenly, my mother's angry face appeared in the window. "You girls get in this house right now and get some clothes on," she yelled as she opened the screen door to let us in.

I immediately felt confined. *I don't want to come into the house*, I thought as I walked up the stairs to the house. *I want to continue running and playing.* But my mother's dreadful expression and voice revealed her anger. I knew my mother would never hurt me, and she never has, yet I was afraid to ever displease her again.

My entire body cooperated in my resentment toward my mother. My face heated up, I thrust out my bottom lip, walked into the house, folded my arms, and plopped down on the floor. *I won't enjoy anything else all day,* I resolved defiantly. (I guess I showed my mother.)

It is not hard to figure out that I like to be free. I love the outdoors. I am also fiercely independent and do not like having people tell me what to do. In fact, each time someone tells me what to do, I feel exactly the way I did when my mother ruined my outdoor romp by telling me to come inside before I was ready.

I also dislike having people angry with me. All it takes is a single look of dissatisfaction to reduce my emotions to those of a two-year-old afraid to anger her mother ever again.

Naturally, my outward reactions rarely reveal my inner unrest. But now that I understand the significance of my first memory, I realize that I have spent much of my life putting effort into being perceived as a "good girl." I am very anxious to please others. I am also a middle child, meaning I often compromise my own needs to earn the acceptance of others. As a melancholic, I judge myself harshly when I fail to be accepted by everyone I meet.

With this profile of myself in mind, let's take another look at my restroom fainting episode on my first day at work, which was described in the last chapter. I wanted to be perceived as a good employee; I wanted others to approve of me. I wanted these things so badly that anxiety eventually caused me to pass out. I even lied to a potential friend so I would not appear weak—and in doing so convinced her that I was one card shy of a full deck. Looking for approval, I received indignation, and I needed a trip to the nurse!

My actions were based largely on my anxiety-prone melancholic temperament. Since then I have also discovered phlegmatic characteristics that have helped me see the problems of being too hard on myself. I learned from my mistakes. The next time my anxiety got out of control, I swallowed my pride and admitted to needing help—before slithering to the ground in another faint.

Many people who suffer from anxiety are insecure due to growing up in dysfunctional homes. Some of the problems that plague such families include alcoholism, excessive drug use, emotional and/or physical abuse, and extreme forms of discipline. Young children sense all forms of dysfunction and respond to them in a variety of ways.

Let's look at Ken's first memory. (Ken is the piano player introduced in the last chapter.) When Ken was five, he was playing with a neighbor child in his front yard when his parents' angry voices suddenly interrupted them. He was used to hearing his parents fight, and he always kept one ear tuned into what was going on—just in case a quick getaway was in order.

"He's just a child," yelled Ken's mother.

Oh no, thought Ken, *They're fighting over me again.*

"That's no excuse for him to mess everything up," answered his father.

Ken's thoughts quickly raced through the day's events. *What have I done wrong this time?*

Suddenly the door flew open as his father came down the stairs and grabbed Ken by the collar. "Get in this house, young man," he yelled as he positioned Ken on the top stair, pushed him into the house, and marched him to his bedroom.

"I thought I told you to clean up your room," said Dad, who had knelt down to be eye level with Ken, who saw his angry glare and smelled the alcohol on his breath.

Unable to withstand the pressure of his father's enraged stare, Ken looked down. "I cleaned it," he said meekly.

Dad pulled Ken by his shirt sleeve into the bedroom. He threw open the closet door and said, "Do you call this clean?"

Looking into the closet, Ken saw the toys he had hurriedly heaped onto the floor so he could go outside and play. *I didn't think he would find them*, Ken anguished.

"I'm sorry," said Ken in shame, fighting to hold back tears. *If I cry, Dad will spank me for not acting like a man*, he thought.

"When I tell you to do something, young man, I want it done right," boomed his father's voice. "Now don't come out of this room until it's perfect."

Throughout Ken's childhood, his father demanded perfection, especially after he had been drinking excessively. Lonely and an only child, Ken never seemed to be able to please his father, though he continued to try. As a melancholic, Ken scrutinized every activity, never able to meet even his own expectations.

The adult Ken is a gifted musician, but also a perfectionist who doesn't want people staring at him. He will not perform at the piano unless he can "play it in his sleep." And his need for approval causes great anxiety, especially when it appears he has failed.

People interpret similar events in various ways, revealing their divergent attitudes toward life that result from birth order and temperament type. Perhaps you remember feeling boxed in or restricted in some way. Kevin Leman and Randy Carlson suggest that such memories may indicate difficulty in dealing with authority. The authors propose that if your first memories are painful and scary, you probably are not a risk taker.

What about a person whose first memories are of loneliness? Leman and Carlson expect this person to have few friends, possibly spending a lot of time reading, watching TV, working, exercising, or involved in similar solitary activities.

At the end of this chapter you will be asked to consider your first memory. This should not be an event that someone else told you about. It should be *your* first memory. If the memory is not like a little movie playing in your head, then it is not yours.

Where were you? What were you wearing? Who was with you? What were you doing? What were the other people doing? How did you feel? Who was in charge? How do these things compare to how you react to your environment today?

As you work through the exercise, dig deep into your memory banks to uncover as many of your earliest memories as you can. Do not worry if the memories do not come easily at first. They are in the corners of your mind someplace. Keep searching. Once you start remembering, you will recall even more memories.

If you dig up a particularly traumatic or painful memory, get it out in the open. Do not hesitate to seek out an understanding, friendly ear. If need be, get professional help!

For example, when 36-year-old Jennifer started remembering her past, she recalled that she had been sexually molested by a trusted relative when she was five. The trauma had been so great that she had suppressed the memory for 31 years. When it finally surfaced, the emotional shock caused intense grief.

Jennifer is an obese woman, standing four feet eleven inches and weighing 325 pounds. Through therapy, she learned that she had used food to cover up the shame of the memory of her molestation. Each tense circumstance Jennifer experienced as an adult manifested the identical response she felt as a molested five-year-old. Whenever she felt anxious, she would head straight for the refrigerator, a fast food restaurant, or the closest vending machine. Jennifer is currently working through her previous trauma by getting in touch with her emotions and learning to express them in ways that do not include food. But her healing would not be possible if she hand't dealt honestly with her memories of early childhood.

Your memories will unveil a lot of information about you. Perhaps your childhood home was not dysfunctional or unhealthy. The source of your anxiety may be difficult to pinpoint. A number of previous incidents may have contributed to your current condition—some which may have seemed insignificant at the time they occurred.

But keep sorting through your memories. They will help you form a mental painting of your life and emotional makeup. And they will help shed light on the root causes of your anxiety.

A word of caution: use the information you discover to understand yourself, and not to make excuses for your anxiety. Your goal should be to *overcome* your anxiety, and this book is one of the vehicles available to help you do just that.

The "Looking Inside" section of Chapter One helped you take the first steps toward understanding your anxiety by putting names, places, and so forth, to your fears.

The "Looking Inside" exercise in this chapter will help you take the second step of placing into perspective some early childhood experiences that may have caused trauma. Identifying the sources of childhood trauma can help you deal with the problems that haunt you even today.

Looking Inside: Evaluating Your
First Memories

1. Listed below are several common causes of unresolved
   anxiety. Check the boxes that describe your life. Use
   the space at the bottom to further personalize your
   list.

❑ I come from a dysfunctional home.
❑ My parents fought often.
❑ My parents divorced when I was young.
❑ I am adopted or lived in a foster home(s).
❑ One or both of my parents had an explosive temper.
❑ One or both of my parents were very strict.
❑ I have never liked one or both of my parents.
❑ I have been told that I experienced some kind of
   accident or severe illness as a baby or young child.
❑ I remember experiencing some kind of accident or
   severe illness as a child.
❑ Someone I cared about died when I was young.
❑ I sometimes feel that I am reliving an experience
   from my past or from a dream.
❑ I have recurring, unsettling dreams.
❑ I sometimes overreact to events.
❑ I do not want to remember my childhood.

Other

2. Describe your first memory, including the people, places, and things involved. (Note: if you cannot picture the event, it is not *your* memory. Someone else probably told you about it. Do not use it).

3. What part of this memory is the *most* vivid to you?

4. Were you in control of the situation, or was someone else controlling you?

5. What emotions did you feel during this event?

6. What did you feel physically during the event?

7. How do your emotional and physical reactions of this memory affect you today?

8. In what kinds of circumstances do you experience similar feelings as an adult?

9. What is the underlying theme of these memories? (Fear? Rejection? Bitterness? Hatred?)

10. If you were an objective observer of your first memory, how would you challenge this child's perception of his or her memory?

11. Based on this new perception, how would you
    encourage an adult with this memory to change the
    way he or she thinks about himself or herself on a
    daily basis?

12. Read Matthew 15:19. What do these verses tell you
    about God's view of how your own thoughts
    contribute to your condition today?

13. Read Colossians 3:21. How does this verse relate to your relationship with your father? Your mother?

14. Read Ephesians 5:22–33 and 6:1–4. How do these standards compare to life in your childhood home?

3

The Home Front

Chapter One helped you begin to understand your anxiety—its nature, the havoc it can wreak in your life, and some of the things you can do to deal with it. Chapter Two helped you understand the forms your anxiety can take. Now the third step toward overcoming your anxiety is to see how your home environment reinforces your emotional turmoil. Just as a deep cut leaves a scar on your skin, life's bumps can leave "bruises" on your soul. This condition is frequently referred to as a broken heart, though there is more to it than that.

Severe anxiety disorders can exist even in loving, Christian homes. They are often the outcome of strictness, misunderstandings, or miscommunication, and they result in unexpressed anger and resentment.

If a person stacks one unresolved problem on top of another for years on end, the burden eventually becomes unbearably heavy. Therapists call this action "stuffing."

A continual stress of emotions in this way is likely to result in an emotional volcano, spewing tears (and sometimes violence) in its path. This kind of damage can be avoided, however. Values, beliefs, thoughts, attitudes, and behavior can expose bruises that are collecting on your soul.

Values: The Foundation of Who You Are

Values are the things you care about deeply, such as ethics, morals, family relationships, religion, and education. They form at a young age as you observe parents and other important role models.

Before I was old enough to go to school, my grandmother created games and songs that (1) were educational, yet fun and (2) taught me about Jesus and the sacrifice He made for me on the cross. She also taught me to sew at an early age, insisting that each seam was straight and precise.

In later years, my mother would meet me at the door every day after school to ask how my day went. While listening, she offered cookies and milk (or something equally delicious) and then sent me to my room to complete homework. Leisure time was spent painting, playing music, or sewing. These hobbies all require precision. My values as an adult now include deep Christian convictions, close family relationships, education, music, enjoying life, and doing a good job in everything I undertake.

In contrast, John was brought up in a different kind of family. His parents were rarely home when he returned from school. Even when they were, John was coaxed outside to play—alone. He ignored homework assignments since his parents showed little interest in his grades. He lived too far from school to participate in outside activities. John's family attended church on Christmas and Easter, but otherwise religion had very little impact in their lives.

John dropped out of school in the tenth grade, following in his parents' tradition. Today his contact with family and friends is minimal. He does not understand all the emphasis Christians give to their religious beliefs, yet he considers himself to be a Christian because he is a good man, rarely breaks the law, and still goes to church on Christmas and Easter. John and I share very few values, largely because we were reared differently.

Defining your values will help determine the impact your beliefs have on your thoughts.

Beliefs: The Trap We Make for Ourselves

Beliefs are the opinions we form of ourselves and of life. We arrive at our beliefs through observation, whether at home as children or elsewhere as adults.

In his book *The Search for Significance* (Rapha Publishing/distributed by Word, Inc.), Robert S. McGee maintains that some people submit themselves to four "false beliefs" that cause them to doubt their own significance. These beliefs motivate fears of failure, rejection, and punishment, and they lead to unhealthy behavior, shame, and hopelessness.

McGee's first false belief is that you must meet certain standards to feel good about yourself. Such a belief prompts a tendency toward perfectionism and a striving for success. It often results in manipulation, risk avoidance, and fear of failure.

McGee's second false belief is that you must gain the approval of others to feel good about yourself. This belief motivates people to unreasonable extremes to please others and makes them oversensitive to criticism. Many people with this belief withdraw from others to avoid the risk of rejection.

A third false belief is that those who fail are unworthy of love and deserve to be punished. This belief inspires a wealth of blaming techniques, including harshly punishing others for one's own failures. Withdrawal from God is a typical response from these people who fear punishment.

The fourth false belief proposed by McGee is that, "I am what I am; I cannot change; I am hopeless." Shame, despair, and hopelessness are the fruits of this belief. It produces passivity, loss of creativity, and isolation.

It is essential to avoid being misled by false beliefs, because a person's beliefs strongly prejudice his or her thoughts.

Thoughts: How You Communicate with Yourself

The thoughts we have about ourselves are frequently referred to as "self-talk" by psychiatrists, therapists, and counselors. The term aptly describes the idea that thinking is how we talk to ourselves.

I often speak aloud to myself when I am in my car or some other place where I am alone. I can more accurately "observe" my thoughts by hearing them. Verbal expression helps me avoid tension-causing thoughts and maintain a positive attitude toward myself and life, no matter what the circumstances.

H. Norman Wright explains that "self-talk initiates and intensifies emotions...self-talk directs the way we behave toward others...[and] determines what we say to others" (*Self-talk, Imagery, and Prayer in Counseling*, Word). He suggests a strong interrelationship between thoughts, feelings, and behavior. According to Wright, "Most of our emotions or feeling responses come from our thought life; what we dwell upon, what we think about, can stimulate feelings."

Experts agree that "what-if" thoughts have a negative impact on a person's emotional health. Negative thoughts are self-defeating and produce equally self-defeating behavior. But since this kind of thinking can become as automatic as driving a car, people may not be aware that they torture themselves this way.

The Scriptures are full of encouragement to help Christians carefully manage their thoughts and lead peaceful lives.

For example, Romans 5:1 and Colossians 1:20 promise assurance of peace with God through His son Jesus Christ. In John 14:27, Jesus offers a peace different than the world offers and exhorts us to not worry or be afraid. Isaiah 26:3 promises peace to those whose minds are fixed on God. And Ephesians 2:14 assures us that Jesus is our peace.

The next time you feel anxious or afraid, consider that God promises to work everything out for your good (Romans 8:28), to supply all your needs (Philippians 4:19), and to equip you to do whatever is required (Philippians 4:13).

Attitudes: Our Measure of Balance

Attitudes are an emotional reaction to the balance (or lack of balance) between our values, beliefs, and thoughts. For example, people who value perfection usually have the belief that they must meet certain standards to feel good about themselves. When self-talk convinces them that they cannot meet such standards, they develop an attitude (or feeling) of fear. Common negative behaviors that might result include overeating, withdrawal, avoiding certain activities, or shifting from one relationship to another.

A supportive, accepting home environment fosters an attitude of acceptance toward ourselves. An abusive home environment (either emotionally or physically) promotes an attitude of harsh judgment toward ourselves and/or others. Lonely environments manufacture people who have difficulty relating to others. Perfectionistic environments, whether in nurturing homes or not, also create people prone to attitudes of harsh judgment. And our attitudes can be changed—or reinforced—by our thoughts.

Pulling it All Together

Values, beliefs, thoughts, and attitudes mold an individual's behavior. Some behavior is constructive, while other behavior is self-defeating. Let's observe how these elements work together using some people you've already met in previous chapters.

You may recall that Ken was an only child with a melancholic temperament and a strong value of perfection. He believed that his performance must fulfill rigid standards in order for him to feel good about himself. He learned this value in an abusive, perfectionist home environment as a child.

Negative thoughts convinced Ken that he could not meet the high standards he had set for himself. A previous failure as a child contributed to this belief, as did parents who did not understand the importance of recognizing Ken's successes. Ken suffered from a high level of anxiety and feelings of inadequacy.

So how was his behavior affected by his values, beliefs, thoughts, and attitudes? He refused to perform. Even after 15 years when hard work seemed to ensure a successful performance, his anxiety left him disoriented and prompted a desire to flee.

Also think back to Vicky with her flashy sports car. Most people buy sports cars to have fun on the road. But Vicky was afraid of traffic. Why would she want a car intended to be driven hard?

Vicky's sports car obviously cost a lot of money, but she did not have a high-paying job. Her clothes were also expensive, attracted a lot of attention, and projected an image of prosperity.

Vicky's behavior indicated the extent to which she valued success. She believed that the approval of others provided a gauge for measuring her merit. Self-talk convinced Vicky that she did not deserve approval. Consequently, she spent beyond her ability to pay so she could appear successful and receive the approval of others.

As a sanguine middle child reared in an extremely dysfunctional home, Vicky's life became an emotional roller coaster. Before she began psychiatric treatment for her frequent panic attacks, she often told herself, *I don't deserve love. God is punishing me for being so sinful. I will never be able to change. My life will always be controlled by panic.*

But Vicky was wrong. So was Ken. The truth is that no one *has* to be controlled by anxiety or panic. *You* make the choice either to control your anxiety or let it control you.

The Truth About Meeting High Standards

If you believe you must meet certain standards to feel good about yourself, consider Romans 8:1. Because you have been acquitted of your sins through Christ, you are pleasing to God. God still disapproves of sinful behavior, but His love for you cannot be shaken.

God will chastise us when we sin—just as a loving parent corrects a child so the youngster will learn acceptable behavior (Hebrews 12:5–11). And according to 1 John 1:9, "If we confess our sins, He is faithful and just to forgive us our sins and to cleanse us from all unrighteousness."

What a relief! I am an OK person not because I met someone else's standards, but because God accepts me just the way I am. God loves me whether my performance is perfect or not. And because of my relationship with Jesus, I can let go of the fear of failure and the tension it causes. Wow!

My life has been transformed by realizing and truly believing these facts. Sure, I still try hard to do the best job I know how, but I no longer kick myself around the block each time I do not meet my own high expectations. As I said earlier, I learn from my mistakes and incorporate the new information into my next try. My heredity, birth order, temperament, and home environment help account for my value of perfection. My thoughts can add to or release me from the tension produced by the value of perfection.

The Truth About Needing Approval

Colossians 1:21–22 dispels the belief that you must attain the approval of others to feel good about yourself. As a Christian, your sins were paid for on the cross and you are reconciled with God. Once you confess and ask forgiveness for your sins, you are fully accepted by God. Some of your behavior may still need to be adjusted, but you *as a person are acceptable to God.*

There is no other way to reach the same level of perfect forgiveness and acceptance. Though you make every human effort to do so, all humans are imperfect. Only God can make you feel completely loved and accepted.

The Truth about God's Punishment

Do you believe God uses anxiety to punish you for some unresolved sin? If so, consider 1 John 4:9–11, which affirms that you are deeply loved by God and that Christ satisfied God's wrath for your sins and failures on the cross.

Romans 3:23 tells us that all people *sin*. It is the nature of mankind. We are not saved from hell because of what we do, but rather by accepting Jesus as personal Savior. If we try to gain acceptance by works, we will fail. Continued failure then thrusts us into an unending cycle of insufficiency, the need to blame others, and anxiety over never reaching our expectations.

If you have not received Jesus as a personal Savior, why not do so now? Confess to God that you are a sinner who wants forgiveness. Thank Jesus for the sacrifice He made to save you from hell. Invite Jesus to be in control of your life. In your mind, bundle up all the ugliness and shame in your life and hand it to Jesus. Leave it with Him, never retrieving it again.

Rest assured that you have no need to fear punishment. And then consider the benefits that will result from your decision: peace, strength, confidence, and all the other wonderful gifts God promises His children.

The Truth about Hopelessness

If you are consumed by shame, hopelessness, or inferiority, consider that you are a new creation in Christ (2 Corinthians 5:17). This newness is also called regeneration, the rebirth we experience when we accept Jesus as Savior (John 3:3–6).

You become a new, beautiful, fresh creature in Christ, perfect and unstained. Ask God to change you, and He will. Then learn to accomplish change through prayer and Scripture reading. (More will be said about these things in Chapter Seven.)

Forgiveness: A Three-Way Mirror

The chief tenet of Christianity is that God loves you. As a Christian, you are forgiven of your sins. Great! So why do you still have anxiety attacks? Maybe you do not fully understand forgiveness.

You may not have *accepted* God's forgiveness or the forgiveness of others, even though it has been offered. Perhaps you have not yet sincerely *asked* the forgiveness of God or others. You may still need to *forgive yourself* for being less than perfect.

Let's take another look at the bruised soul concept presented earlier in this chapter. A soul bruise is the outcome of emotional abuse, whether real or perceived. Bruises can occur in loving, nurturing environments as well as in dysfunctional or abusive settings.

For example, I remember bringing home a near perfect report card. The only imperfection was a single B (in math, my most dreaded subject). With a huge smile, I proudly handed the report card to my mother, ready to receive lavish congratulations and praise.

My mother jokingly asked, "What caused you to mess up so badly?"

My heart fell. I thought, *How could I have been so stupid as to believe this was good enough?* My face stung with embarrassment. I wondered, *Was my sister's report card better than mine? I've disappointed Mom again.*

My mother, who showed love and concern for me on a daily basis, accidentally bruised my soul. She did not abuse me; she jokingly said something that I allowed to hurt my feelings. Believe it or not, it took me years to forgive myself for getting that B in math—or my mother for pointing it out. To this day, I do not like being teased about my performance. Fortunately, I have given up holding grudges for years on end. It takes too much energy.

Jennifer, the overweight sex-abuse victim introduced in Chapter Two, also suffers from a bruised soul. The causes of her bruise are more serious, and the effects are more debilitating. The end result, however, is the same: anxiety.

I react to anxiety with hard work. Jennifer responds by eating. Forgiveness is a healthier option for both Jennifer and me.

Forgiveness can heal the bruised areas of *your* soul as well. After sensing God's forgiveness in your own life, it's up to you to forgive others who may have offended you in some way. But sometimes it's harder than usual to forgive others. Or you may think you have forgiven when you really have not, which was the case after my report-card incident. It took me months, even years, of reflection to realize that I still needed to forgive my mother for her casual comment.

I finally understood that because I try so hard to please people, I find it difficult to admit failure or ask for help. Therapy helped me get in touch with the pain caused by this bruise—and many other bruises I picked up along the way. After therapy and encouragement from others, I was able to get rid of some of my performance-oriented behavior, which relieved much anxiety. I have not had a fainting spell in over ten years.

Jennifer's situation is different. Her abuse had a much more significant impact on her self-esteem. She felt dirty and shameful. She ate to cover up those feelings, and she did not even remember the abuse until 30 years later. Her therapists are helping her learn to uncover suppressed memories, understand and exercise atrophied emotions, forgive her abuser, and release the shame that consumes her. The supernatural strength and love of Jesus Christ is helping her experience forgiveness.

Matthew 18:21–35 suggests that God forgives us to the extent that we forgive others. Galatians 5:16–26 tells us that an attitude of forgiveness achieved through a spiritual walk with the Lord results in the fruit of the Spirit: love, joy, peace, patience, kindness, goodness, faithfulness, gentleness, and self-control.

Chapter Four will delve more deeply into the topic of forgiveness, the plague of negative emotions that result from unforgiveness, and the destructive behavior that ensues.

The following "Looking Inside" exercise will help you uncover possible areas of unforgiveness in your life. As you answer the questions, try to remember any abuse that may have caused bruises to your soul (emotions, mind, and will). These are the events that blend with your values, beliefs, and thoughts to cause feelings of fear and an attitude of anxiety.

Looking Inside: Evaluating Family and Peer Relationships

1. Describe your relationship with your father.

2. Describe your relationship with your mother.

3. Describe your relationship with your siblings.

4. How did you get along with peers at school?

5. Describe your relationship with the friends you have today.

6. If married, describe your relationship with your spouse.

7. If you have children, describe your relationship with each one.

8. Describe an event that caused you to doubt your self-worth or feel inadequate.

9. Describe an event that caused you to feel guilty for some reason.

10. What is your greatest need?

11. From whom do you receive love?

12. Looking back at your relationships and interactions, what people and events cause you to feel angry?

13. What do these relationships and feelings reveal about your beliefs and thoughts?

14. Read Colossians 3:13–14. What does this tell you
    about your *responsibility* to forgive (either yourself or
    someone else)?

15. Read Romans 8:26–27. What does this tell you about
    your *ability* to forgive?

16. Read Galatians 5:16–26. What does this tell you about
    the *rewards* of a forgiving heart? About the conse-
    quences of unforgiveness?

4

Dirt Clods in Your Furrows

As the process of understanding anxiety continues, most people begin to recognize the methods they use to sabotage themselves. So the next step is to identify and eliminate self-destructive behavior. Some such behavior is obvious: excessive drinking, smoking, drug use, and even attempted suicide. These actions are indeed harmful. But so are many other seemingly benign behaviors.

In his book *Codependency* (Rapha Publishing/Word, Inc.), Pat Springle explains that it is self-defeating to lose objectivity. Overresponsibility is detrimental. Putting up emotional walls or attempting to control others damages us. Harboring negative feelings toward another person can place us at the mercy of our emotions.

Take Denise for example. After 20 years of marriage, Denise's husband, Nick, had an affair with another woman, Sharon. As if that were not bad enough, Sharon was Denise's best friend. Sharon justified the relationship,

citing Nick's unhappiness and saying he needed a friend
to talk to. Her interest prevented Nick from working things
out with Denise.

Denise wanted to save her marriage and demanded
that Nick reject Sharon, using extremely unkind words.
But when it became obvious that Nick was not willing to
stop seeing Sharon, Denise's emotions got the best of
her. In a number of separate meetings, Denise graphically
described the full extent of her hatred for both Nick and
Sharon. She also vowed never to tell Nick anything about
their eighteen-year-old daughter, Jamie. If Jamie wanted
a relationship with Nick, she would have to pursue it
herself. *I will neither encourage nor discourage it*, she
determined.

Jamie was as angry as Denise. She rarely attempted
to call her father. But she never explained that this was
her choice, not Denise's, so Nick blamed Denise for
Jamie's behavior.

During the next three years, Denise reconstructed a
happy life for herself. She remarried, pursued a new
career, and solidified her relationship with God.

But she could not forget about the wrong done her
by Nick and Sharon. *I don't know what I would do if I
ever ran into one of them,* she agonized. These thoughts
haunted her at work. While driving, her eyes constantly
searched for Nick's or Sharon's car. She never entered a
restaurant or shopping mall without first anxiously
scanning the parking lot.

One day as Denise left one store in a mall, she
noticed Sharon and her daughter shopping in another one.
Denise flinched as if hit in the face. Her heart began to

race and her entire body trembled. *I have to get out of here!* she thought. She left the mall immediately and ran to her car, as if fleeing a wild animal.

Denise's panic was the result of attempting to run from the anxiety caused by her ill will toward Sharon and Nick.

You cannot eliminate anxiety by running away. It will affect you until you deal with it. Running away causes the significance of the offending person, place, or thing to be blown out of proportion. But facing your fears lets the air out of inflated apprehension.

Denise prayed, *Please help me forgive Nick and Sharon.* Still, each time she thought of them, tension and depression converged upon her. She continued to pray, read the Bible, and learn all she could about her emotional dilemma until one day she had a dream.

Overlooking a field of corn she had meticulously planted, she proudly noted the neat, straight furrows. Large, green plants flourished as they absorbed nourishing water into their roots.

But something was preventing the water from reaching the plants down the row. Some obstruction caused large pools of water to spill from one furrow into another, leaving the plants beyond unhealthy and limp. Confused, Denise searched for the source of the problem. "What's wrong?" she wondered aloud.

A deep voice gently said, "Clean the dirt clods from your furrows."

When the alarm clock awoke Denise, her mind quickly shed its morning cobwebs. The meaning of her dream grew increasingly evident. She thought, *I've harbored feelings of bitterness and hatred toward Nick and Sharon. Even though I've felt justified, I now realize that my negative emotions have provoked behavior that has hampered a portion of my life. I can't enjoy a meal out or a shopping trip—two things I used to love. I'm always thinking about the events that led to my divorce, even though I'm happier now than I've ever been before.*

While dressing for work, Denise gazed at herself in the mirror. Like a lightening bolt from the sky, she was hit by one of those blinding recognitions of obvious truth: *I haven't felt God's forgiveness for my divorce because I haven't forgiven Nick and Sharon!*

Driving to work, Denise wrestled with how to respond to the message of her dream. *I created ugly scenes expressing my hatred and bitterness,* she thought, *these are preventing my continued growth.*

"Sharon, Nick, I'm sorry," she said aloud as she drove through rush hour traffic. "I had no right to try to hurt you that way."

Tears stung her eyes. She realized, *I have to call each of them to apologize.* (Denise had moved out. Nick and Sharon still lived where they had three years ago.) The idea of calling terrified her.

"I cannot call them," she said to God. "They hate me. They will never hear what I have to say. They don't even recognize how much I have been hurt by what they did."

Throughout the day, Denise's thoughts continued to focus on Sharon and Nick. And in the weeks that followed, she grappled with her personal conviction that she must call. Before long the emotional turmoil began to affect her concentration and creativity.

"They are the ones who should offer an apology," she pleaded with God.

I'm dealing with you now, was the response she sensed.

Denise arrived at work early one Thursday morning, determined not to put off the call any longer. Her trembling hand dialed Sharon's number. After three years, she could still remember the number.

The sound of Sharon's ringing phone incited fear. *She hasn't answered,* Denise thought. *I could hang up. No one would ever know.* Denise had the same impulse to run that she had felt when seeing Sharon at the mall.

"Hello," said Sharon's friendly, expectant voice.

"Sharon, it's Denise." It felt as if her heart stopped as she waited for a response.

"Yes," said Sharon, as if spitting out bad tasting medicine.

Denise boldly continued. "I wanted to let you know...I have been thinking a lot over the past three years. The events of a few years ago were...all so ugly. And you probably view what happened differently than I do. I wanted to tell you that I no longer have any hard feelings toward you. If I caused you pain, I'm sorry."

Denise closed her eyes, awaiting Sharon's reply. *I really blundered that,* she thought. *I hope I managed to get at least some of my point across.*

"I'm surprised and amazed," Sharon answered. "Why did you choose now to say this?"

"Because it isn't healthy to dislike someone or know that someone else dislikes you." Denise's tongue tripped over her teeth as she spoke. Every fiber of her body trembled, affecting her voice.

"I don't go around wishing bad things on you, if that's what you're worried about." Sharon's disdain for Denise still permeated her voice.

"No. I just wanted you to know that I no longer have hard feelings toward you." With closed eyes, Denise prayed, *Please give me the right words to make Sharon understand.* She continued, "I have often wondered what I would do if I saw you on the street. I can now say that I would like to stop and talk to you, like a regular person."

"I can't say I am there yet," answered Sharon. "Once I have said good-bye to someone, I like to keep it that way."

"Oh, me too," answered Denise, sensing the weight of miscommunication. "I am just trying to release both of us from the burden of how I have been feeling about you."

"OK," answered Sharon hesitantly. "How's your life?"

"I'm extremely happy," said Denise, her thoughts turning to her new husband and the beautiful life she now enjoyed. "And you?"

"I'm fine," Sharon said, though her voice sounded anything but fine.

"Sharon, I wish you all kinds of happiness in your life."

"Thank you," said Sharon, her voice losing its tautness. "And to you."

They hung up. Denise felt a torrent of racing emotions, and she tried to identify each feeling. Had the call made a difference? Was she in God's will? Could she now get on with her life?

Suddenly Denise realized, *Sharon never asked for my forgiveness. Doesn't she know how wrong she was to force me out of my marriage? Doesn't she care that she hurt me?*

"Did I do the right thing?" Denise asked God.

Tranquility gently enveloped her. A genuine sense of release followed. But later she thought of Nick and again she began to tremble.

"God," she desperately prayed. "He hates me. He hurt me. I'm not ready to forgive him. He was my husband, and he traded me in like a used car. I'm a person. I was his wife!"

Clean the dirt clods from your furrows.

Her office phone rang. *Thank you, God*, thought Denise. *Saved by the bell.* The busy day that followed kept Denise from thinking more of Nick.

But after a sleepless night, Denise got up early. She drove to work, ready to call Nick and practicing what she would say. *I'll make it clear that I still believe he did wrong. I'll only apologize for having negative feelings toward him. Well, maybe I should also apologize for standing in our backyard screaming hateful words—loud enough for the entire neighborhood to hear.*

She dialed his number, thinking, *This used to be* our *number.* Denise knew Nick would still be home. After 20 years of marriage, I know his habits.

No answer.

That's strange, she thought. *Maybe he's changed as much as I have.* She called at lunch time. Still no answer. She called again after work.

"Hello," said Nick.

Denise's heart leaped into her throat. Her mind went blank as she said, "It's Denise."

"What do you want?" he asked harshly.

"I want you to know that I no longer have any hard feelings toward you."

"OK," he answered. "How's Jamie?"

I vowed never to tell him anything about Jamie. What should I say? The answer became immediately clear. *I have to clean all the dirt clods from my furrows, including self-defeating vows made in the heat of anger.*

"She's fine," answered Denise. "I told her that if she wanted you to know anything about her, she would have to tell you herself."

"I haven't heard from her in months," said Nick bitterly.

"She's happy," answered Denise.

"OK. See you later," said Nick abruptly.

Click. Buzz.

The surrounding air seemed heavy. *He's the one who had an affair. He rejected both Jamie and me. Why does he blame me? Dear God, why does he blame me?*

Nick and Sharon will have to answer to God themselves. She flipped to Galatians 6:7. *We all reap the harvest of our own lives.* She looked at Galatians 5:16–26. *Unforgiveness keeps us prisoners to our emotions. Thank you, God, for helping me forgive them.*

In following God's leading to express her forgiveness, Denise was released from the burden of her negative emotions. *I can almost feel the dirt clods of hatred and bitterness dissolving.* She had done all she could do and the situation was in God's hands. His love could now flow into all areas of her being to create healthy, spiritual growth.

Defense Mechanisms

Hide and Seek—We humans have amazing ways of defending ourselves. When someone wrongs us, we become angry. The response is natural and healthy. Yet hanging on to that anger is self-defeating. Anger can become a cancer that destroys our self-esteem, the ability to function, and our relationships.

How do you think Denise's unreleasd anger affected her new husband each time she refused to go to a restaurant because Nick or Sharon might be there? By hiding from the source of her anger to avoid facing it, Denise was causing unrest with him.

Another common defense mechanism is denial. Denise denied that her anger was a problem. She rationalized that Nick and Sharon were to blame for what happened. She felt she had nothing to apologize for. However, the forgiveness we receive may very well depend on the forgiveness we offer others (Mark 11:25).

Negative feelings toward others act as dirt clods in the furrows of our lives, denying us from receiving certain spiritual benefits. Denise robbed herself of peace until she chose to forgive. Once she expressed forgiveness, she felt a sense of release. The dirt clods dissolved as God provided a clean, nutritious supply of water to the furrows that were previously dry.

If your life seems to be enveloped by trouble, examine your behavior for clues to a solution. Even if circumstances have worked against you, your attitudes and methods of dealing with problems can make a world of difference in the outcome. You can choose self-destruction, or you can choose a better option.

Looking for Love—Love is a basic human need. But too many people abuse and misuse "love." For some, it becomes another defense mechanism. Some jump from one relationship to another, looking for the kind of excitement that eventually died in the last one. Others become puppets to the people they love, doing and saying exactly what they think the other person wants them to. This desperate behavior causes a loss of personal identity—and probably a resentment of the object of one's affection.

All the while, these people feel inadequate, maybe even unlovable. They wonder what is wrong with them, why they cannot stay in love, why people do not stay in love with them.

The answer is found in Matthew 22:37–39, where Jesus gives us two commandments relating to love. First, we are to love God with all our hearts, souls, and minds. Second, we are to love our neighbors as we love ourselves.

An intimate relationship with our Lord Jesus Christ taps us into the only kind of love that can make human relationships work. Peace with God allows us to have peace with others. Through a relationship with God, we receive (and learn how to give) unconditional love, the only level of love that creates lasting relationships with other people.

Closeness to God also reveals many of the defense mechanisms we have developed that sabotage our relationships. When we feel unlovable, we sometimes try to prove we are right. We become perfectionists, acquire a sharp tongue, heap guilt upon ourselves and others, judge or scold others for imperfections that we also possess, or race from one unfulfilled relationship to another.

These defense mechanisms are intended to help you avoid the pain of potential rejection by having the other person(s) sense your rejection first. This system allows you to feel justified in blaming the other person for the failed relationship. You then continue to sink deeper into the slime of self-pity and self-flagellation, tightening the anxiety-causing strings that control your life until they become a noose around yourself.

Life in the Fast Lane—Some people try to avoid anxiety by always being busy, never taking time to reflect upon their real feelings. But they cannot hide under a mountain of activity forever. Their feelings will eventually catch up with them. It is good to regularly take a moment from your job, committees, and social life for introspection.

Remember that Jesus' instructions were to love God with all your heart, soul, and mind. He didn't add, "and with every ounce of energy you have, even at the cost of

your health and family relationships." His command to
love our neighbors as ourselves can never be carried out
effectively until we learn to love ourselves. Our health
and relationships are important to Him.

When God leads you to serve Him, do it. But
sometimes it is necessary to quietly wait upon the Lord
for the wisdom to identify the dirt clods that keep you
from receiving His total blessing, and for the courage to
arouse and feel the prickle of numbed emotions you find
hidden in the deep corners of your being.

Drowning Your Sorrows—Many people try to avoid
their feelings through the use of drugs and alcohol. This
is a course headed for self-destruction.

In their book *Your Parents and You* (Rapha
Publishing/Word, Inc.), Robert S. McGee, Jim Craddock,
and Pat Springle explain that "the fact that a person would
use [drugs and alcohol] to numb himself, while being
aware of the chemical's destructiveness, can only
demonstrate how desperate a person may be to end his
pain."

Many self-help and professional treatment programs
are available for people plagued with addictions. Some
of these programs are listed in the Appendix.

Eating Disorders—I cannot count the number of
times I heard disturbing news and headed straight for the
refrigerator. After downing a pie, I would head for the
store to buy muffins, only to think, *That did not do the
trick. Mashed potatoes might make me feel better.* But
no, I just felt bloated—and ashamed.

I am not significantly overweight, so it was difficult for me to see the connection between my overeating and my hidden emotions. Many people overeat to cover up feelings. It is a problem I continue to struggle with. However, because I now understand what causes me to overeat, I have learned to ask myself, *What feeling am I attempting to suffocate by stuffing this pie into my face?*

Honesty works. Give it a try. It is better to face and deal with emotions rather than destroy your body and self-esteem by overeating.

Other forms of eating disorders include anorexia and bulimia. Anorexics refuse to eat. Bulimics binge and then purge. Both disorders put strain on body functions—and if not dealt with will eventually result in death. They are both slow, torturous suicide. Psychiatric treatment is required to overcome these disorders.

Methods for understanding and reacquainting yourself with your own emotions are presented in the next chapter.

The following "Looking Inside" exercise will help you identify destructive behavior, the role you play in failing relationships, and some choices that can turn your life around.

Looking Inside: Destructive
Behavior Inventory

1. Check the box next to the characteristics that describe
    you. Use the space at the top of the next page to
    further personalize your list.

❏ I sometimes enter into relationships that I know are
    harmful to me.
❏ I often feel that my relationships are one-sided, with
    me putting more into them than others do.
❏ When others criticize me, I believe I deserve it.
❏ I hide facts about myself that would cause others to
    stop liking me if they knew.
❏ I get frustrated when others do not do things my way
    or take my advice.
❏ I have been described as a perfectionist.
❏ I find it difficult to say "no."
❏ I fear loneliness.
❏ I give either too little or too much attention to my
    appearance.
❏ I cannot seem to find time for prayer and Bible study.
❏ My habits of eating, exercising, and sleeping are
    inadequate.
❏ I thrive on change and/or crisis.
❏ I avoid play and vacation time.
❏ I avoid friends and family.
❏ I hold others responsible for my present condition.
❏ I avoid conflict, even if it means my feelings or
    opinions may be disregarded.

❑ I avoid risking the rejection of others.
❑ I display compulsive behavior (frequent house
   cleaning, hand washing, drinking, etc.).

2. Describe the events surrounding the most recent
   breakup of an important relationship (whether
   friendship, love relationship, job, etc.).

3. What role did you play in this breakup?

4. How were you wronged in this relationship?

5. Describe other situations in your life where the pattern described in the above relationship resembles other break-ups in your life.

6. If a friend described a similar problem to you, how would you challenge his or her view of the victimization?

7. Read Proverbs 13:20. What can you do to form relationships that will enhance, rather than tear down, your self-image?

8. Read Philippians 4:6–8. How can your self-talk (the things you tell yourself) change your self-image and the way you look at life?

5
What is a Feeling?

Now that you have begun to understand the nature of anxiety, it is time to move on to the next—and most important—step: overcoming it. Conquering fear will require making friends with your emotions, forming positive relationships, and leading a balanced lifestyle.

Emotions are always present, whether or not you feel them. This chapter will help you initiate the process of making friends with your emotions. Later chapters will help you learn to use them constructively.

Sometimes the problems of life convince us that it is safer to withdraw emotionally than to allow ourselves to feel our emotions. We don't want to be vulnerable to other people, so we deny our feelings. But there is a problem here.

Feelings are a package deal. Emotional withdrawal doesn't just suppress negative emotions; it eliminates positive ones as well...things like the joy of playing hide and seek, the satisfaction of doing nothing on a day off, or the pleasure of having sex with your spouse.

In the restroom on my first day at work, it would have been more productive to tell the woman, "I feel so anxious for acceptance that I fainted." Maybe she would have understood the need of a young woman to be liked by her coworkers. She probably would have helped me off the floor, straightened out my "dress for success suit," and offered a hug. "I understand," she might have said. "I felt that way my first day, too. Would you like to have lunch with me?"

It would have been a relief to have had lunch with a new friend that day. But I will never know what the woman might have said or how she would have reacted to my true emotions. I denied myself the possibility of having her friendship—and in the process caused myself to look silly.

Take a moment right now to recall times you have denied yourself the privilege of feeling. Perhaps you have rendered yourself unable to identify your emotions—or to feel anything at all.

In her book *Codependent No More* (Harper & Row), Melody Beattie says:

> We frequently lose touch with the emotional part of ourselves. Sometimes we withdraw emotionally to avoid being crushed. Being emotionally vulnerable is dangerous. Hurt becomes piled upon hurt, and no one seems to care. It becomes safer to go away. We

become overloaded with pain, so we short circuit to protect ourselves.

An Emotional Time Bomb

As Beattie suggests, "stuffing" is a survival technique. We sacrifice our own interests and activities for others so we can avoid conflict or feel accepted. We stuff so much resentment and anger within ourselves that we become a time bomb about to explode. We are in danger of erupting and spewing forth a lifetime of negative emotions at any moment.

In *The Courage to Heal* (Harper & Row), Ellen Bass and Laura Davis offer advice specifically to adults who were victims of child sexual abuse. Though not a Christian book, it does contain an excellent chapter on coming to terms with your own emotions.

Bass and Davis concur that, "We have feelings all the time, whether we are aware of them or not." The authors say that our emotions are responses to whatever is happening. "A threat makes us fearful. When something injures us, we feel hurt and angry. When we are safe and our needs are met, we feel content."

Do You Stuff Emotions?

In my book *Life Doesn't Have to Hurt* (Thomas Nelson), I described an easy way to determine if you stuff emotions:

Think about when and how you show anger. For example, do you seem to maintain control over

yourself most of the time and then "fly off the
handle" at little things? If so, you are suppressing
your anger (and being unfair to yourself and the
person at whom your anger is directed).
It is much easier for someone to understand a firm
yet loving verbal expression of anger at the time
you feel offended. Abusive language or behavior
when you have finally "had enough" is much more
difficult to accept, or forgive.

Bourne describes other symptoms of suppressed
feelings. These include free-floating anxiety (described
in Chapter One), depression, psychosomatic illness, and
muscle tension.

Try to recall a time you were anxious but did not
know why. Perhaps you thought you needed to take action,
so you changed something, anything—your job, your hair,
your mate, where you lived, or any number of things.

A better response would be to take time to figure
out what you are feeling and why. Techniques for
accomplishing that feat will be described later in this
chapter.

Once you understand what you are feeling, action
may indeed be necessary. In that case, carefully plan
what you need to do and proceed with confidence. We
will discuss emotions in regard to decision making later.

Who is to Blame?

Perhaps you can trace your "stuffing" tendencies to
an unhappy family situation. If so, you probably
discovered as a child that it was unsafe to be angry, so

you refused to feel anything at all. Since then, you may have come to blame any number of things for your stuffing—your childhood, your spouse, the stress of your job or family life, or even the loudness of thunder.

Stuffing occurs in happy homes as often as unhappy ones. Anyone who begins to think, *I should not feel the way I do,* learns to believe that his or her feelings do not matter. Environments that deny the privilege of expressing true emotions render people unaware that many such emotions even exist. The discomfort brought on by not knowing what they are feeling causes anxiety.

Add to that a great chasm between values and belief systems, and the result is a situation that is generally all out of whack.

Succumbing to the message that feelings do not matter causes people to feel trapped each time they are in danger of exposing emotions. They may feel backed into a corner or out of control. Their bodies react to the possible chaos of expressing genuine feelings, and their level of anxiety is increased.

Anxiety is a reaction to our inner feelings. Does this mean we are responsible for our own anxiety? Melody Beattie contends that "when we feel happy, comfortable, warm, and content, we usually know all is well in our world, for the present moment." But when we feel uncomfortable, "our feelings are telling us there is a problem."

To identify the problem, we must understand what our emotions are telling us. We must continually read our emotional barometers, which is not possible when hiding from our feelings.

So yes, we are responsible for our own anxiety. There is no need to go on blaming anyone or anything. Cut through your excuses, identify what is *inside you* that causes anxiety, and deal with it.

Emotions and Decisions: A Balancing Act

A word of caution is necessary at this point. According to Beattie, "Our feelings can trick us too. Our emotions can lead us into situations where our heads tell us not to go."

This poses a dilemma. We are supposed to allow ourselves to acknowledge our true feelings, yet it is possible for our emotions to mislead us. So how are we supposed to know if our anxiety is warning of a bad decision, or even if the absence of anxiety indicates all is well?

The answer to this dilemma is to let God be your guide. Good decisions are always based on His counsel, received through prayer and Scripture reading.

Effective decisions are made after gathering all available facts, discerning what data applies to your specific situation, and then seeking the counsel of God and possibly trusted friends. The final decision should always be based on whether it will glorify God, not on whether it will impress others.

Once you have made a responsible decision, it is time to take action. Step out in confidence, knowing that God is in control. Release yourself from the anxiety about whether or not you made the right decision. Hand everything over to God.

Hello, I am a feeling

If anxiety has been a problem for you, it's time to quit going through life pretending you do not have feelings—or allowing your emotions to send you flitting in the wind as if you were a feather. Stop hiding your anxiety attacks. Stop blaming your current predicament on past circumstances.

By now you should understand the cause of anxiety: emotional overload. Apply that knowledge to your life. Identify and take charge of your negative or out-of-control emotions. Use them to understand yourself and to thwart your anxiety.

Face your feelings honestly. Beware of confusing beliefs with emotions. ("I feel my boss dislikes me.") Beliefs come from the head. ("My boss dislikes me.") Emotions come from the heart. ("His unjust treatment makes me feel unliked.")

As you identify your feelings, your list will probably include both negative and positive words. Positive feeling words include: amused, accepted, content, happy, relaxed, and worthwhile. Negative feeling words include: afraid, angry, ashamed, desperate, guilty, hurt, insecure, lonely, pressured, stupid, unfulfilled, and worried.

Read the previous lists of feeling words aloud. Use various intonations and observe the sensations the words

induce. Use appropriate words from this list and add others
of your own as you complete the "Looking Inside"
exercise at the end of this chapter.

Learning Healthy Ways to Express Emotions

Many people have no difficulty expressing anger.
The problem is that they cannot control the ways they
express it. In some cases, these people become so angry
that they lose touch with their positive emotions. They
need to learn healthy ways to express the full continuum
of their emotions.

For other people, expressing *any kind* of emotion is
difficult because they have had little practice. They have
suppressed their emotions for so long that they no longer
recognize what they are feeling.

Keeping a diary is a good way to get in touch with
your emotions. Pay attention to your behavior, noting the
physical sensations attached to certain actions. Attach
emotion words to your behavior and physical sensations.
And when an emotion pokes its head up from under the
rubble you have piled on top of it for all these years, do
not run from it. *Feel* it!

My friend Vicky used to say, "I think I'll go crazy if
I let my emotions surface." But she started attending an
anxiety support group where she met other people who
had the same fears—and many who had overcome them.
She learned that people rarely go crazy just because they
allow themselves to feel. They may hurt for a while. But

Vicky's group had discovered that feeling good *most* of the time is better than never feeling anything at all.

If you are numb from years of not allowing yourself to feel, think about how someone else might react under the same conditions. Keep in mind that heredity, birth order, temperament, and environment make your emotions unique to you. Each of us is unique in what we feel and why we feel that way. But as you imagine what others might feel, you may come up with some clear insight into your own previously hidden feelings.

Creative activities also help us get in touch with our feelings. Music has worked well for me. I needed to teach myself to "go with" my feelings rather than squelch them, so I learned to express myself by either singing or dancing to especially moving songs. I also write about my feelings.

Creative expression is not the same as performing. Do not worry if you cannot carry a tune in a bucket, if you have two left feet, or if your poetry stinks. It is just for you.

Remember that the sensation of stirred emotions might be scary at first. If that happens, take a time out. Breathe. Call a friend. Listen to relaxing music. Pray. Hug your pillow. Do whatever works for you. If you are prone to panic, plan how you'll get yourself through the panic *before* it happens.

In time, you can restore your feelings without the accompanying fear. And you can take the risk of feeling good again. Take it slowly. Be ready for anything. If you tap into old rage, find healthy ways to express it, perhaps in group therapy or some other support group.

You may also find, as I did, that you are suddenly more prone to crying. More things move me to tears now—watching graduations, holding a baby, getting my feelings hurt. But that is OK. It is a wonderful part of feeling the fullness of being me.

Keep feeling and expressing. Once you get through the initial stages, the uncontrollable tears will subside. If not, there are many places to seek help. Names and addresses of the national offices of a few support groups appear in the Appendix. By all means, do not lock yourself back into a closet of unexpressed emotions.

Take the Plunge

Anxiety is a choice. You can continue to stuff emotions compactly inside until anxiety overtakes you. Or you can choose a more healthy route by turning your emotions from adversaries into allies.

As Ellen Bass and Laura Davis say, "Learning to tolerate feeling good is one of the nicest parts of healing" (*The Courage to Heal*, Harper & Row). They suggest taking note of the things that induce positive feelings in order to "take the risk of admitting that you feel good—first for a moment, then for longer."

Use the following "Looking Inside" exercise to identify your feelings, their sources, and your methods of dealing with them.

Looking Inside: Feelings Inventory

1. Describe the physical response you have when you allow yourself to experience the following emotions.

Anger

Resentment

Abandonment

Jealousy

Foolishness

Hurt

Happiness

Energy

Positive

2. What circumstances bring out each of these feelings in you?

Anger

Resentment

Abandonment

Jealousy

Foolishness

Hurt

Happiness

Energy

Positive

3. When do you believe you need to suppress each of these feelings?

Anger

Resentment

Abandonment

Jealousy

Foolishness

Hurt

Happiness

Energy

Positive

4. Read 1 Peter 5:6. If anxiety is a symptom of your attempts to control your situations, how can you best handle your anxiety attacks?

5. Read Philippians 4:6–7. How can you cast your anxiety upon God?

6. Use the following pages this week to keep a diary of events, your feelings about those events, and your physical reactions to those feelings. (If you have not been allowing your emotions to surface, record the way you think you *should* respond to each of the events in your life.) At the end of the week, review your diary and look for patterns.

Day 1
Significant events:

My feelings (or the way I think others would feel in my shoes):

My physical reactions to the feelings (or lack of feeling):

Day 2
Significant events:

My feelings (or the way I think others would feel in my shoes):

My physical reactions to the feelings (or lack of feeling):

Day 3
Significant events:

My feelings (or the way I think others would feel in my shoes):

My physical reactions to the feelings (or lack of feeling):

Day 4
Significant events:

My feelings (or the way I think others would feel in my shoes):

My physical reactions to the feelings (or lack of feeling):

Day 5
Significant events:

My feelings (or the way I think others would feel in my shoes):

My physical reactions to the feelings (or lack of feeling):

Day 6
Significant events:

My feelings (or the way I think others would feel in my shoes):

My physical reactions to the feelings (or lack of feeling):

Day 7
Significant events:

My feelings (or the way I think others would feel in my shoes):

My physical reactions to the feelings (or lack of feeling):

Patterns I have displayed this week regarding which emotions are most prevalent and how I deal with them:

Steps I will take next week to help myself turn adversarial emotions into positive feelings:

6

Liking Yourself

You've begun to understand what causes anxiety and what you can do to prevent it from ruining your emotional stability any longer. You have learned to uncover feelings that may have been buried for years. Now you may find that the next step you need to take is learning to like yourself.

In this chapter, you will learn that liking yourself requires inner peace, which is also an antidote for loneliness and anxiety.

When you become comfortable with yourself, many of the sources of your anxiety will disappear. That is not to say you will never again feel anxious, but the intensity of your anxiety attacks will decrease and your methods of dealing with fear will be more effective.

How to Like Yourself

As Robert S. McGee revealed in *The Search for Significance* (Rapha Publishing/distributed by Word, Inc.), developing a positive self-image has little to do with gaining the acceptance of others or performing to high standards. Rather, it is based on liking yourself—warts and all. We cannot establish and enjoy healthy friendships if we have no love for ourselves.

You took an important first step toward liking yourself by picking up this book and reading this far. If you were plagued by anxiety and fear, you should now be able to recognize and admit that these feelings have had a negative impact on your life. And you can now begin to develop self-love.

The people whose stories have been told in this book have learned to love themselves. How? By realigning their belief systems so they could receive fulfillment from experiencing God's love.

Love Yourself Through God

As Robert McGee has said, people cause themselves anxiety when they look to performance-based relationships for self-worth. It is hard to be on stage all the time, and we do not have to! Inner peace is possible through a personal relationship with Christ.

This was a lesson Andy had to learn. When he was in college, he tried hard to perform well in everything he did. He put in long hours as he attempted to get good grades, hold down a part-time job, maintain lots of friendships, and keep in touch with his family.

Andy's devotion was admirable, but he developed a nervous problem. His hands shook constantly. He had trouble sleeping. He began losing weight. He wanted to run, but he did not know where he would go or why he wanted to escape. He wondered, *Am I losing mind? I can't tell anyone about these weaknesses*. I must act like a man. He chose to suffer in silence, all the while wondering what was "wrong" with him.

At church, Andy began to notice an older man who looked to be in his late 70s. The old man's gray hair handsomely framed a pleasant face with bright eyes that had, through the years, lost some of their deep blue color. Yet those eyes were still beautiful—not so much because of their physical characteristics, but because of how they looked at people.

Andy's young heart saluted this older man for the happy tranquility he radiated. In a conversation with his pastor, Andy said, "I want what that man has."

"What would that be?" asked the pastor with a friendly smile.

"I was hoping you knew," said Andy out of his emptiness. "Something about him is...different. He's nice to be around. He seems happy with himself and everyone else. I'll bet he's never had a sad day in his life."

"He's had plenty of sad days," laughed the pastor. "But wouldn't you say he seems peaceful?"

"Yes!" said Andy with excitement. "Peace is what he has that *I* want. And it is what I'll have when I graduate, get married, have a good job, buy a big house, and start a family."

"Peace does not come from material possessions or outward circumstances," said the wise pastor. "It originates from an inner relationship."

Andy was too caught up in a flurry of activity to understand. Robert McGee calls this a "performance trap."

His relationship with God consisted of church on Sundays and a hurried prayer before drifting off to sleep. He was too busy performing the activities he thought would lead to success to establish a close affiliation with God. The more he tried to perform, the farther away from God he felt—and the larger the spiritual void within him became.

It would take Andy a long time before he slowed down enough to comprehend the importance of loving God with all his heart, soul, and mind. As much as he wanted inner peace, it would be many years before he would allow God to supply it.

We will follow up on Andy later. At this point, just be assured that peace and self-love are available to all of us. Let's take a closer look at the characteristics of a peaceful person.

Characteristics of a Peaceful Person

Peace is a gift to us from God through Jesus Christ (John 14:27). Consequently, it makes sense to focus our attention on Jesus rather than on circumstances. You can thank God for your circumstances when you accept that He knows what is best and are convinced that He will work everything out for your good.

I knew I had finally learned how to accept God's gift of peace when a coworker said, "You have an amazing ability to remain completely unflappable in the most unnerving of situations."

Me? The one who used to faint at the mere thought of meeting new people?

When inner peace comes from a personal relationship with Jesus Christ, peace in our friendships will then follow. We avoid restless, anxious people. We know how they feel, and we do not like it. But when we see someone who possesses inner peace, we immediately want it too.

Peaceful people look for ways to resolve conflict, not cause strife (Matthew 5:9). They accept that all things work together for those who love God (Romans 8:28). They exude confidence that God will supply their every need (Philippians 4:19). And they realize that *needs* are not equal to *wants*.

The strength of a peaceful person comes from knowing that the power of Jesus is sufficient to do whatever is required (Philippians 4:13). They are confident that peace is possible based on Psalm 29:11: "The Lord will bless His people with peace."

Have you allowed the trials of life to deny you peace? If so, consider the instructions and the promise found in Philippians 4:6–7:

> "Be anxious for nothing, but in everything
> by prayer and supplication, with thanksgiving,
> let your requests be made known to God;
> and the peace of God, which surpasses all
> understanding, will guard your hearts and
> minds through Christ Jesus" (NKJV).

When I finally got tired of fainting several times a month (each time something upset me), I decided to find a way to calm myself. I started praying for peace: *God, I know You didn't cause this hardship, but I can't handle it. Why aren't I good enough for You to protect me? What have I done to displease You?*

Then I started looking at my situation differently. Instead of believing I was born to be a victim, I began to search for the opportunity for improvement provided by each adverse situation.

Eventually I became able to thank Jesus for the lesson I would learn from each problem. I also got excited about the possibility of helping someone else through a similar situation.

It seems strange to thank God after fainting and hitting my head on the floor, but that is exactly what I started doing. I soon learned that fainting was the result of letting too many unimportant things get to me. (I already knew my fainting spells weren't a sign of a brain tumor, epilepsy, or some other debilitating disease. Several doctors had told me I had none of these illnesses.)

If you suffer from fainting or similar outward symptoms, do not discard the possibility of some physical problem. But also consider that it may indicate an inappropriate perspective on life.

You can panic and lose control in tense situations. Or you can look for the opportunity to learn from what is happening—and thank God for it. The latter is much more productive.

Finding Peace

Remember that you can expect to find peace as you learn to love God with all your heart, soul, and mind. You will not find peace in money, fancy cars, or performance-based relationships. I have already looked. Perhaps you have too.

I find that prayer and meditation on the Scriptures fortifies my self-image, builds my faith, and strengthens my intimacy with God. Time alone with God is the most profitable time of my day. Whenever I have to miss that time, I feel as if I lose out on something valuable.

But some people will probably disagree with me. There are those who do not find peace through their relationship with God. This happens occasionally when people do not have the correct image of God.

Through self-talk, some people convince themselves that God is harsh and punishing. Others can accept that He loves them and wants to give them peace. You can see your circumstances as a learning ground and an opportunity to grow, or you can get angry at God and continue to live in anxiety. It is your choice.

But since people without peace are critical, quick to anger, and negative about life, they repel those who have a positive outlook. If you want to form healthy relationships, you need to attract healthy people. That means you need to *choose* to be healthy so you can display a peaceful demeanor.

Content to be You

I will always remember the day I found contentment with myself. Looking through my Bible, I was trying to discover why God kept me from being rich. I wanted to buy things and live in a big house. I thought it was unfair to have to work so hard for everything. In general, I was wallowing in self-pity.

Then I discovered 1 Timothy 6:6–8, and my heart stirred with excitement. I felt like a cartoon character whose eyes jumped right out of her head and onto the page as if they were on springs. I am sure they must have made a *boing* sound. Here is what I read: "Now godliness with contentment is great gain. For we brought nothing into this world, and it is certain we can carry nothing out. And having food and clothing, with these we shall be content."

I had found the answer! God knows how much income and opportunity I can handle and still depend on Him. Satan wants me to focus on what I cannot have, fostering a virus of discontent. And once I stopped focusing on what I did not have, I started noticing what I *did* have. I lived in the richest country of the world. I had always had enough to eat. I was healthy.

That very day I made a list of 10 things for which I was thankful. I praised God every day for those 10 things. My list soon grew to 20 things, then 30, and eventually to the point where I do not even keep a list. I am now content with all that God has given me.

I am still not *financially* rich, but that is OK with me because the Bible says that love of money will leave us spiritually unfruitful (Mark 4:19). I have discovered the extent of my *spiritual* wealth, which is far more satisfying. As a result, I like myself and I can have peace through faith because God assures me that *anything* is possible (Mark 9:23). He can and will do whatever is necessary for me. It is up to me to follow where He leads. If I choose to follow His guidance, then my circumstances will be fulfilling.

The people who used to be attracted to me were not emotionally healthy—neither was I. But since I have developed genuine inner peace, that has changed. I now attract a different kind of people—those who are also peaceful and content.

Accept God's all-encompassing love and do not worry about living up to the expectations of others. Many people will not appreciate the fact that you are happy when they are not, but that is a problem for them to resolve with God. It is not your concern.

Strengthen Your Strengths

Someone once advised that to feel comfortable with my own weaknesses I needed to strengthen my strengths. I tossed this advice aside. I thought, I need to eliminate my weaknesses so no one will ever be justified in criticizing me. Silly me.

It is certainly all right to try to strengthen some of our weaknesses. But if we try to eliminate *all* weaknesses, we set ourselves up for anxiety!

For example, I practically drove myself crazy trying to alter my quiet nature. I tried performing—in front of people. During a gymnastics meet in high school, my backside shook so hard my friend described it as Jell-O. Later in life, a high-visibility, high-stress job left me so confrontational by the end of each day that my family decided it was safest to avoid *all* contact with me. Was I lonely!

I do not like being in front of crowds, and I knew it. Yet I wanted so much to perform well *in everything* that I pushed myself into situations I thought would strengthen my weaknesses. Instead, I wiped out all my self-esteem. I also neglected building up my strengths. Consequently, I became a mediocre person until I accepted my weaknesses and started to work on my strengths. As I began to strengthen my strengths, I was surprised how many weaknesses just disappeared—or became unimportant.

The Bible tells us that success is not measured by what we have. Rather, it is measured by what we do with what we have (Matthew 25:21). What we do with our strengths and weaknesses will help determine how successful we become.

I am now comfortable giving a presentation, but I don't enjoy it. I prefer putting others up in front—the people who *want* that kind of attention. My current career in public relations is working out much better than anything else I have ever done. I diligently look for the right press opportunities for my company, and then I find the right person to fill the need. I can stay in the background, and still make sure things go as planned.

I discovered that my quiet nature is not a weakness. It allows me to listen to everything that is going on around me and to notice details that many other people do not. Instead of kicking myself for being quiet, I have developed my quietness as a strength. I am succeeding, and it feels good.

What are your strengths? Identify them and exercise them. You may be surprised to find that many of what you perceive to be weaknesses are really strengths if you find constructive uses for them.

You will fail occasionally. We all do. But failure is a stepping stone to success. It is a normal part of life. Failing is not an indictment that you are a *failure*.

Loving Others as Ourselves

Back when I used to let other people walk all over me, I justified it to some extent by quoting the Golden Rule: "Do unto others as you would have others do unto you" (based on Matthew 7:12).

Yet I did not want to be walked on. Why should I let others take advantage of me? If I wanted people to accept me as I was, what good did it do to constantly deny how I was (quiet)? How could I expect others to be comfortable with me if I was not even comfortable with myself? But after I learned to love myself, I could love others in the same unconditional way. Loving others as ourselves means we must first love ourselves—deep inside. Boisterous, cocky people do not love themselves. They are insecure and try to hide who they really are. It is hard to be around such people who do not even like being around themselves.

The Power of Prayer and Meditation

I want to emphasize that prayer and meditation on the Scriptures are important elements in learning to like yourself. Through the Scriptures you learn that you are perfectly pleasing to God, no matter what worldly standards you fail to meet. The moment you accept Jesus as your Savior, you become reconciled with God. The opinions others have about you become inconsequential.

No sin is so great that Jesus cannot forgive it. No fear is too terrible for Him to handle. You can let go of your anxiety, turning it over to Jesus through prayer and meditation. In its place you can experience the soothing fruit of the Spirit as outlined in Galatians 5:22–23: love, joy, peace, patience, kindness, goodness, faithfulness, gentleness, and self-control. You'll never make a better trade.

Looking Inside: Realigning Your Belief System

1. Check the box next to the characteristics that describe you. Use the space after Section D to further personalize your list.

   A. Characteristics of False Belief #1: (*I must meet certain standards in order to feel good about myself*).
      - ❏ I fear failure.
      - ❏ I am a perfectionist, especially when it comes to my own performance.
      - ❏ I am driven to succeed.
      - ❏ I find myself manipulating others in order to achieve success.
      - ❏ I avoid healthy risks, but sometimes take risks sure to fail.

   B. Characteristics of False Belief #2: (*I must have the approval of certain others to feel good about myself*).
      - ❏ I fear rejection.
      - ❏ I attempt to please others, no matter what the cost to myself.
      - ❏ I am overly-sensitive to criticism.
      - ❏ I withdraw from others—whether through secrecy or aloofness—to avoid disapproval.

C. Characteristics of False Belief #3: (*Those who fail, including myself, are unworthy of love and deserve to be punished*).
- ❑ I fear punishment and do what I can to avoid it.
- ❑ I find ways to punish others.
- ❑ I look for blame for my failures.
- ❑ I have withdrawn from God and other believers.

D. Characteristics of False Belief #4: (*I am what I am; I cannot change; I am hopeless*).
- ❑ I harbor feelings of shame, hopelessness, or inferiority.
- ❑ I have become increasingly passive about my circumstances.
- ❑ I seem to have lost my creativity.
- ❑ I feel isolated and alone.

Other characteristics I display:

2. Read Romans 5:1–8. Explain why you are perfectly pleasing to God, no matter what worldly standards you fail to meet.

3. Read Romans 5:9–11 and 8:38–39. The moment you accept Jesus as your Savior, you become reconciled with God. Explain how this reconciliation renders the opinions of others powerless.

4. Read 2 Corinthians 5:21. What sin is so great that Jesus did not already pay for?

5. Read Romans 8:1–17. By what power can you put
   away your spirit of fear?

6. Read 1 John 4:17–18. What does it mean to be perfect
   in love?

7. What steps can you take to realign your belief system
   with the truth through Jesus Christ? (Forgive yourself?
   Accept your weaknesses? Strengthen your strengths?
   Spend more time with God? etc.)

7

Developing Positive Relationships

When anxiety strikes, it helps to have a trusted friend you can call on...someone who will listen attentively to your reasons for being upset and then lovingly talk you down off the ceiling.

I once had to wait three days to be interviewed over the phone for a nationwide radio program. I found out about the interview on Friday afternoon. It was scheduled for the following Monday. Many people would consider a wait of this kind to be a tense situation. I know I did. I had all weekend to convince myself that I would completely bungle the interview—and what a superb sales job I did on myself!

I expected the call at 1:00 p.m. on Monday, but the phone remained silent until 1:45. When it finally rang, the voice asked to reschedule the interview for 2:30.

"Sure," I said with complete confidence. But after replacing the phone, I fell to pieces.

I am going to forget everything, I told myself. *What if I get the statistics wrong? What if I stutter? I am going to blow it, I just know I am!*

While I feverishly scrambled to write down every statistic I could find that related to the interview topic, my dear friend Vicky called.

"I am having a nervous breakdown," I said in a panic. "I have to go."

"Calm down and tell me what's happening," she said, concerned.

After I described my dilemma, Vicky calmly said, "Go get your Bible and read Psalm 91."

"I'm too busy," I said bluntly.

"No, you are not," she insisted. "It will help."

I obeyed. After reading the Scripture, I smiled and thought, *I'm doing exactly what I constantly tell Vicky not to do. Self-talk catapulted me into a full-blown anxiety attack. Vicky brought me back to earth.*

All anxiety sufferers need a friend like Vicky. But to have such a friend, you must first be one. Sound relationships require the development of healthy ties and the efforts of both parties to keep the friendship strong. Unhealthy alliances are not worth the toll they take on your emotional well-being.

In this chapter, we explore the differences between healthy and unhealthy relationships. We will look at ways to avoid unhealthy ones and maximize healthy ones.

Unhealthy Relationships

In his book, *One-Way Relationships* (Thomas Nelson), author Alfred Ells defines one-way relationships as those in which one person consistently:

- Puts more into the relationship or takes more responsibility than the other person
- Modifies his or her behavior out of apprehension about what the other may say, do, or feel
- Avoids honest, open, and loving communication with the other person
- Presumes the other's incentives or actions
- Conceals the truth, offers excuses, or rationalizes another'sunacceptable behavior
- Criticizes, blames, or exhibits negativity toward the other person
- Wants to fix the other person or persuade the person that he or she is wrong
- Keeps the peace at any price
- Loses emotional stability with the other person's moods
- Feels addicted to the other person or the relationship
- Always acknowledges mistakes and apologizes first
- Works harder to make the relationship succeed.

We met Andy in the last chapter. Andy had a one-way relationship with his father. No matter how hard he tried, he could not seem to please his father, who tried to act as he thought he should in regard to "being a man." The father rarely hugged Andy. He never said "I love you." He demanded that Andy hold his hurt inside—so Andy too would "be a man."

Andy's father meant well. It's not that he wasn't a good man. But because Andy regularly tried and failed to please his father, the relationship caused Andy more sorrow than happiness. It was definitely unhealthy for Andy.

As a result, Andy had no peace. He stuffed his feelings and tried very hard to perform to extremely high standards, some that were self-imposed and others that were expected of him. His "dislike" of himself was stronger than his "like."

Andy had difficulty communicating his feelings, which caused problems in forming intimate friendships. Lack of communication is a key ingredient for a failed relationship, whether between friends, spouses, or children.

Sometimes it is necessary to take an inventory of the people we know who are bad for us. In some cases, you and the other person will be willing to work to improve the relationship, and it is good to do so. You never know how valuable some friendships are until they fail. However, if some of your relationships continue to harm you, no matter how hard you try to correct the situation, it may be best to end them.

Sometimes a particular relationship is harmful to your physical or emotional health, but you cannot seem to end it. If this is the case, you may be addicted to the other person. Codependency support groups might provide the help you need. If not, you may need to seek professional help.

What Makes a Healthy Friendship?

Friends accept one another as they are. They listen to each other, encourage one another, and talk through any problems in the relationship. Anything less is not a healthy friendship, and it will wear you down rather than build you up.

Friendships form when two people share common attitudes. Age and backgrounds may be completely different, as long as the attitudes are compatible. Two people may both be 30, from Colorado, and from loving, middle class homes, and they still might not get along. Yet a 30-year-old can be the closest of friends with a 60-year-old or a 10-year-old, as long as they share compatible attitudes. The 30-year-old also needs friends his or her own age, but the friendships with the 60-year-old and the 10-year-old can be equally fulfilling.

Love between a husband and wife is friendship with an additional erotic dimension. Friendship between spouses is a requirement for any happy, satisfying marriage. Similarly, parents can be friends with their children (though this is best accomplished *after* the children have left home and the parents no longer have to play authority/disciplinary roles).

For example, the love I have for my daughter is much different than my love for my beloved husband, and both are different than my love for Vicky. My daughter is married and lives in another state, yet we share a deep friendship marked by love and open communication that allows us to smile and feel comfortable. We share ideas and feel free to express opinions, whether positive or negative.

Healthy friendships improve our physical, emotional, and spiritual lives. Unhealthy relationships detract from them.

How to Form Healthy Friendships

Friendships require time and energy. They withstand problems such as conflict, envy, and hurt feelings. Though intimacy is not the reason to make friends, it often becomes a by-product. Here are some suggestions to help make good friends:

- Take a fearless look at your past relationships, examining both the good and bad ones.
- Risk communicating your needs and desires to others, maybe even discussing your conclusions about past relationships with someone else. Do not push for intimacy, but allow it to happen naturally. Do not avoid closeness with someone because you fear rejection.
- Learn to communicate openly and honestly, and look for friends who will do the same.
- Know and respect your boundaries and the boundaries of others.
- Pray that God will bring people your way who are emotionally healthy—then accept each person as is.

If your network of personal friends is limited, look for a support group in your church or other community organization. Vicky, for example, attends Anxiety Anonymous meetings. She has several friends in this group who understand the severity of her panic attacks—they've been there. They help each other through difficult times. (A listing of several support groups appears in the Appendix.)

Biblical Counsel about Friendships

The Book of Proverbs is full of good advice for forming healthy relationships. For example, Proverbs 27:6 tells us that "Faithful are the wounds of a friend, but the kisses of an enemy are deceitful."

I think this means that when we look for healthy friendships, we should avoid people who are brimming with empty flattery. We need to find those we can trust to be loyal and honest, who can lovingly tell us when we have messed up. Such friends reduce our anxiety levels.

I am not talking about people who constantly criticize because they are insecure and want to bring us down to their level. We need friends who are content with themselves and are happy to allow others to be content with themselves as well. They are not always trying to change others to meet their own standards.

As mentioned in the last chapter, a personal relationship with Jesus taps us into the only kind of love that will make our human relationships work. We should start looking for friends by looking first to God, being ever mindful that He works through others for our development. Confidence in a relationship with Jesus allows us to cope with rejection from people.

The Role of Prayer

An excellent example of loving prayers between friends is found in Philippians 1:3–11. In this passage, Paul prays that his friends will receive love, spiritual knowledge and enlightenment, and other spiritual benefits.

The Bible tells us to pray—for ourselves and for others. We are even given instructions on *how* to pray. For example, the Lord's Prayer (Matthew 6:9–13) teaches us that prayer should include a number of aspects, such as praise, adoration, thanksgiving, affirmation, supplication, forgiveness, and renewal.

In prayer, do you give honor to God for who He is (the one who can cure your anxiety) and what He has done (loved you)? This component of prayer is called praise. Jesus gives us an example of how to give God praise in the words, "Hallowed [or revered] be Your name."

Affirmation is a concept that involves agreeing with—and submitting to—God's perfect will. Jesus uses the words, "Your will be done on earth as it is in Heaven." When we fool ourselves into believing what we want rather than what God tells us, we add to our stress. Knowing God's will comes through a healthy diet of prayer and Scripture reading. Following His will is an act of trust that He knows what is best for you—including the kinds of friendships that will strengthen, not deteriorate, your spiritual life.

The third aspect of the Lord's Prayer is supplication, or asking for things. ("Give us this day our daily bread.") Jesus tells us to ask for whatever we need (Matthew 7:7).

God is a loving heavenly Father. He knows what is best for us. The answer to some of our requests is, thankfully, no. But often we discover many of the benefits of not getting what we asked for.

Forgiveness is the next principle found in the Lord's Prayer. ("And forgive us our debts, as we forgive our debtors.") To remain in perfect harmony with Him, we must confess our sins, ask His forgiveness, and accept His loving pardon. If you have sincerely confessed and asked forgiveness of a sin, He has already forgotten it. There is no need to keep bringing it up. You are free of the debt to God, because Jesus paid the price for that sin on the cross. Do not insult God by refusing to forgive yourself. Also remember to forgive others in the same way that God forgives you (Matthew 6:15).

Another component of prayer is renewal, or regularly seeking God for help in resisting temptation. ("And do not lead us into temptation, but deliver us from the evil one.") You are not a sinful person if you feel tempted to do something wrong. Everyone is tempted. The problem comes in giving in to the temptation. Also, if you have a habit you would like to stop, you feel stress each time you succumb to it. God will see you through any temptation, but an active prayer life is a vital component of fulfilling this need.

Finally, Jesus teaches us to close our prayers in a way that glorifies God. ("For Yours is the kingdom and the power and the glory forever. Amen.")

How do your prayers stack up against the model Jesus gave us? Do you *believe* that God will deliver you from your anxiety attacks? Or is prayer simply a technique you use to calm yourself down?

Do you accept God's answers to your prayers, even when He responds in ways other than what you wanted or expected? Remember, He is the one in control, not you. He is the only one qualified to determine how to answer your prayers.

Finally, we should not try to manipulate God by suggesting how He should answer our prayers. Some people pray, "Use me in a big way," when it would be more appropriate to simply pray, "Use me."

Jesus is our source of living water (John 4:10). He will provide for us and give us peace, joy, and love—the traits that help us like ourselves and form healthy friendships. If you were to compare your prayer life to a cup with which you receive God's living water, would you be able to do so? Or would the cup be filled with holes due to ignorance of the Scriptures leading to a lack of trust and honesty, both with yourself, others, and God?

A cup full of holes won't hold much water.

Neither can a prayer life provide the peace and security you need if your own actions continue to make you feel unloved and unblessed.

In an attempt to be perfect—a perfect employee, a perfect spouse, a perfect parent, a perfect friend, a perfect Christian—do you become more anxiety ridden than ever before? A basic knowledge of Scripture will release you from the need for perfection and strengthen your relationship with God. Only then can you know freedom from anxiety.

Looking Inside: Plugging the Holes
in Your Cup

1. What excuses do you offer to God for your actions?

2. What causes you not to trust God?

3. Using the following Scripture, begin a renewal of your prayer life. But before you begin, sit quietly for a few minutes, clearing your mind of everything but communicating with God.

   A. Read Romans 11:33. Quiet your spirit, think about many of the things God provides, and then enter into prayer, bringing praise, adoration, and thanksgiving to Him.
   B. Read Psalm 25:4–6. Continue your prayer by asking for God's guidance in your life. Then quietly wait upon the Lord and accept His will in gracious obedience.

C. Read Hebrews 4:14–16. Ask God for what you *need*. Then trust Him to do what is best for you.

D. Read 1 John 1:8–9. Confess the sins God lays on your heart, ask for forgiveness, accept His forgiveness, and then remove those sins from your mind forever.

E. Read Ephesians 6:10–11. Pray for strength to stand against today's temptations. (Repeat this part of the prayer throughout the day as needed.)

F. Read Psalm 27:13–14. Close your prayer by expressing glory to God.

4. What can you do to strengthen your prayer life on a consistent basis?

8

It Ain't Gonna Reign No More

The final step in overcoming anxiety is learning how to relax and live a balanced lifestyle. This chapter examines various relaxation techniques.

Learning to Let Go

You cannot begin to relax until you let go of the past. Realize that the things that have happened have happened, and you cannot change that fact. All you can do is go on from here.

You may have been abused as a child, betrayed by a trusted friend, or seriously injured in an auto accident. Whatever the problems of your past, it does no good to hang on to past grief. Choosing to do so is a decision to let anxiety reign in your life, so stop trying to control and manipulate people and situations. Such attempts only lead to anxiety. So let go!

Understand and Respect Your Own Phobias

Another aspect of relaxing is admitting, understanding, and respecting your fears. If you are afraid of spiders, be honest about it. If driving across town frightens you, don't try to hide that fact.

Do not do what Vicky used to do. She would make plans to meet me somewhere and then make excuses for having to cancel. After starting her recovery program, she now says, "I'd like to see you, but I am still too afraid to drive that far."

Honesty is a much better solution for your problems than constantly making excuses for your behavior. I no longer resent Vicky for cancelling so many of our plans. She no longer feels guilty for having to hurt my feelings or lie to me. This new arrangement causes less anxiety for both of us.

Think It Through

When caught in the throes of an anxiety attack, it may be difficult to think clearly. Yet that is exactly when clear thinking is most needed. You may be surprised at the number of anxiety attacks you attribute to one thing when they are really something else.

Decide if your fear is justified or if it is something you invented. If evidence suggests fear is warranted, take action. If no evidence exists, examine the situation and determine the real cause of your anxiety.

For example, perhaps you feel neglected by your spouse or family. You begin to fear they will reject you, so you distance yourself from them by criticizing and attempting to control them. Your behavior is intended to manipulate your family into paying more attention to you, but it has the opposite effect. A healthier approach would be to tell your family that you are feeling neglected and afraid they are going to reject you. When the problem is out in the open, at least other people are able to help you with it.

It is important not to allow your anxiety to defeat you without a fight. Rather than quitting your job because you might get fired, discuss your performance with your boss. Instead of cutting all your hair off because you have nothing better to do, examine the reason for your need of attention. Before you eat that eighteenth chocolate chip cookie, think about what void you are trying to fill—and what better ways you could choose. In other words, think the problem through before you act.

Plan Ahead

Anxiety makes thinking difficult, and panic compounds your confusion. So plan how you will get through your next panic attack. Make a list in preparation for it. For example, your list may include suggestions such as:

1. Take a deep breath.
2. Call a friend (Phone number:).
3. If that friend does not answer, call someone else (Phone number: _____).
4. Reread Chapter Eight of *Conquering Fear*.
5. Read your favorite passage in the Bible (Page number:).
6. Pray.

7. Skip rope.
8. Hug your teddy bear.
9. Eat 10 crackers. (Count them.)
10. Listen to your favorite song eight times.
11. Write down 10 ways to make this the best year of your life.
12. Go to a quiet place to be alone temporarily. (Have one in mind ahead of time.)

Decide what calms you. Remember that you are not going crazy. Believe that your feelings will not harm you. Understand that you will eventually get through your panic attack. Do not pump up your fear by running. Accept the feeling of panic as something that is part of you. Above all, stick to your Panic Plan.

Breathing and Relaxation Exercises

Anxiety causes muscles to tighten and breathing to become irregular. Edmund Bourne writes that: "Under tension, your breathing usually becomes shallow and rapid, and occurs high in the chest. When relaxed, you breathe more fully, more deeply, and from your abdomen" (*The Anxiety and Phobia Workbook*, New Harbinger Publications). Shallow breathing restricts oxygen to the brain which induces the foggy, unreal feeling that accompanies panic. Several exercises can teach you to relax your muscles and control your breathing.

Practice abdominal breathing daily. Lie comfortably on the floor with your hands on your abdomen. Inhale through your nose, allowing your abdomen to move as your chest rises and your lungs become full. Hold your breath for three seconds. Exhale through your mouth while you check for any muscle tightness. Consciously relax tight muscles as you repeat this exercise 10 times.

When anxiety strikes, think about your breathing. Rather than allowing yourself to slip into shallow, panicky breathing, sit straight. Deeply inhale through your nose, hold the breath for three seconds, and then force the air out through your mouth. To relax muscle tightness, slowly raise your arms over your head as you inhale. Lower them as you exhale.

Staying Fit

Stretching and exercising your muscles as you breath helps calm you. The better your physical health, the better able you are to withstand anxiety. Aerobic activities such as walking, jogging, swimming, and bicycling offer both enjoyment and improved fitness—even for former champion couch potatoes.

You know when you are out of shape. If walking up a flight of stairs leaves you gasping for air, strolling around the block renders you unable to get out of bed the next day, or your daily routine leaves you in a state of tiredness, lethargy, or boredom, then you need to get more active. However, these symptoms may also indicate other health problems, so consult your physician before beginning any exercise program. And whatever activity you choose for getting back into shape, make sure it is something you enjoy.

I do not believe in the "no pain, no gain" school of exercise. The only thing I gain when I am in pain is an intense desire to stop whatever I am doing. Pushing too hard may cause muscle damage. When you exercise, start slowly and build up to a more strenuous workout.

A good exercise program includes five minutes of stretching, five minutes of slow warm-up activity, 10 to 30 minutes of faster aerobic activity, and five minutes of slower cool-down activity. For example, if your chosen aerobic activity is walking, stretch your leg muscles before leaving home. Walk slowly for five minutes, then quicken the pace. Begin with a 10-minute fast walk. Over a period of weeks, work up to 30 minutes of fast walking. Then slow your pace for five minutes to avoid muscle damage. You should feel refreshed and relaxed at the end of your activity, not exhausted and in pain.

To maintain your motivation, keep a record of your progress. Set goals for yourself and reward yourself for meeting each goal.

You Are What You Consume

Stimulants such as caffeine, nicotine, and certain drugs do exactly what the name implies: they stimulate you, aggravate anxiety, and trigger panic. Salt, preservatives, and sugar are other substances that can stress your body. Some foods may also induce allergic reactions such as anxiety, moodiness, insomnia, headaches, and confusion.

I once had a headache that lasted months. After three doctors told me I had no headache, I went to an allergist.

"Don't eat dairy products, sugar, or yeast," he said.

"What else is there," I asked with a slight chuckle.

"There are the food groups you learned about in elementary school," he laughed. "Try eating breads with no yeast, fruits, vegetables, meat, poultry, fish, beans, and nuts."

I had to plan meals carefully to eliminate dairy products, sugar, and yeast. I also ate out less often and cut down on canned and prepared foods. But my headache disappeared within a week. And even better, I felt more alert, less tired, and had fewer of the PMS symptoms that had plagued me for years.

If you suffer from anxiety, find out if you have any food allergies. Eliminate stimulants and reduce your intake of sugar, salt, processed foods, and animal fat. Increase your intake of fiber, fresh fruits and vegetables, and water (6 to 8 eight-ounce glasses per day). Consult your doctor about whether you need vitamin and mineral supplements.

Soothing Music

Music has a powerful impact on most people. Keep a library of soothing music that can help you relax. I find instrumentals most effective, though many hymns contain lyrics that specifically address anxiety, such as "Tell It to Jesus," "What a Friend We Have in Jesus," and "Love Lifted Me."

Memorize the words to hymns that contain a message that helps relax you. Try singing them to yourself when anxiety or panic seizes you. (You may sing silently if you are riding in an elevator or doing something else in a crowd.)

Wait on the Lord

I asked Vicky, "What is the most effective thing a person could do to overcome anxiety?"

Without hesitation, she answered, "Pray."

As you learn to pray effectively, God will reveal things you do to cause yourself anxiety. It is a process that takes time.

Be patient. As Hosea 6:3 says, "As surely as the sun rises, He will appear; He will come to us like the winter rains, like the spring rains that water the earth" (NIV).

God wants you to experience His loving peace. When He offers that peace, acknowledge and accept it.

Scheduled Worry

Your anxiety will not disappear overnight. But you can begin to control it rather than letting it control you. Make a list of all the things you worry about ("Worry Items"). Schedule a regular time to think about your Worry Items, then forget about those things the rest of the time. Whenever one of your Worry Items pops into your mind, remind yourself that you will worry about that at your specified time. Mentally push that item out of your way and go on with your day—in peace. You may discover that many of your Worry Items lose their significance when you control them in this way.

Experiencing Peace and Joy

A balanced lifestyle is key to experiencing the peace and joy available through your relationship with Jesus Christ. As you begin to overcome anxiety, you will need proper nutrition, exercise, sleep, play, and quiet time with God. Your new lifestyle should include friends who share common attitudes with you, forgiveness and re-evaluation of yourself, and continuous faithful response to God's leading.

You will never be completely free from anxiety. We all experience some form of anxiety from time to time. But you *can* choose how future attacks will affect you. If you choose correctly, peace and joy await.

Looking Inside: Action Plan

1. List actions you can take to control your anxiety rather than letting it control you.

2. List your Worry Items.

3. What day and time will you set aside to worry about these items?

4. What will you do if your Worry Items enter your mind at any time other than your scheduled Worry Time?

5. List your Panic Plan.*

6. Read Psalm 91. What encouraging things can you tell
   yourself the next time fear overtakes you?

APPENDIX A

Treatment Options

Treatment options consist mainly of group therapy, outpatient counseling, and inpatient treatment.

Group Therapy

Group therapy provides a nonrestrictive atmosphere and a safe environment where you can talk about your anxiety with others who struggle with the same kinds of problems. Led by trained therapists or peers, group participants relate their experiences and offer love and support to one another. Meetings provide a structured way to examine and correct what is wrong.

Not all meetings are alike. Look for the one that best suits your needs—and then stick with it. It may hurt at times, but you must get through the pain before you can find the peace.

Rapha offers small group materials and training for a wide variety of needs, including: self-esteem issues, depression, chemical dependency, codependency, eating disorders, and other emotional and relational problems.

Group therapy works for many. Others need more structured settings.

Outpatient Counseling

In outpatient counseling you meet individually with a trained therapist. The private setting makes many people more comfortable than group meetings, though it does not offer the advantage of comparing stories and solutions with other anxiety sufferers who can assure you that you are not alone and that your condition is treatable. Many people combine outpatient counseling with group meetings.

Although outpatient counseling is generally more costly than self-help groups (which are usually free), many clinics offer a variable fee schedule.

Inpatient Treatment

Inpatient treatment offers a safe setting for dealing with your anxiety issues on an intensive level. Programs vary in duration and techniques. Carefully select an inpatient program that best meets your needs. Your local telephone book may list various centers. Call all of them, asking specific questions about their treatment and philosophies.

Reputable centers offer education, individual therapy, group therapy, and family therapy to help patients understand and modify their lives. Other treatment sometimes includes therapies such as psychodrama, art, music, and recreation.

Spirituality is an important aspect of any treatment program. When searching for a group, counselor, or inpatient setting that is right for you, ask questions about their meaning of the word *spiritual*. If Christian is what you want, request a Christ-centered program. "Spiritual" does not always equal Christian.

Rapha is the nation's largest provider of Christ-centered in-hospital treatment care. Their programs address mental, physical, and spiritual needs to help clients learn how to deal with life by not basing their self-worth on their performance or the opinions of others. They also help churches to establish support groups, providing training materials, video and audio tapes, and books. They have programs throughout the country. For more information on their programs, write Rapha at 8876 Gulf Freeway, Suite 340, Houston, TX, 77017, or call 1-800-383-HOPE.

The Use of Medications in Treatment of Anxiety

In both outpatient counseling and in-hospital treatment programs, sychiatrists may treat severe cases of anxiety with medication. Be aware that the use of medication should always accompany counseling to help you uncover and deal with the underlying issues that cause your anxiety. Without the counseling, the use of medications is merely pulling a veil over your emotions—your problems will not go away. The use of some drugs without counseling can only intensify the situation.

The types of drugs most commonly used for anxiety are tranquilizers. It is your responsibility to understand the side effects of any drugs prescribed to you. Consult your doctor or a library. Tranquilizers can be addictive and should be used for short periods of time, and only if your anxiety is disabling.

Antidepressants also are used to combat anxiety. These generally are nonaddictive and are most commonly used for people who experience panic with their anxiety attacks.

APPENDIX B

How to Start and Run
a Support Group

Support groups are effective ways for anxiety sufferers to gain insight and guidance from others with the same problem. If you are unable to find a group that fits your needs, you may want to consider starting a group.

The purpose of a support group is to provide a loving, accepting environment for people to look deep within themselves. Openness and honesty are the strengths of a good support group. The leader's role is to facilitate discussion. Participants should feel safe to become vulnerable to one another.

Group facilitation does not require a degree in counseling, psychology, or social work, though such credentials can help. More important is the ability to communicate and listen. You need to possess sensitivity to the needs of others. You need to be able to discern when defense mechanisms are in use. You need the ability to draw people out of themselves. If you have ever led a

Bible study group or other discussion, you may already possess these skills.

It is not the role of the facilitator—or the group—to become an "armchair counselor." Instead, the role is to promote discussion and prayer. The goal is to help others reflect on their lives, learn to apply biblical principles and overcome the debilitating effects of anxiety.

Prayer is a priority in finding group participants, setting the agenda, deciding on discussion topics and homework assignments, and preparing for each meeting.

Where Are All the People?

Your church may be a good place to start looking for group members. (Try to find at least five participants.) Before the first meeting, determine the expectations of yourself and each group member by asking the question, "What do you want to get out of this group?"

If it appears all prospective participants have similar expectations, you may be ready to get started.

What Is the Group's Level of Commitment?

God can work in any group. Exciting things happen in groups where everyone shares a sincere desire for diligent study and accountability to one another. As the facilitator, your prayers and enthusiasm can help instill these traits into your group.

There will always be people who only want to observe others, and who rarely participate themselves. The facilitator should give these people every opportunity to enter into the discussion by asking open-ended questions or requesting their specific opinions. Remember, many anxiety sufferers consider their opinions to be worthless. They will be reluctant at first to share them. Affirm their responses to encourage them to open up.

Another way to help strengthen each participant's level of commitment is to allow different people to prepare for and introduce each week's topic. Anyone who takes this responsibility will be struggling with the anxiety that brought them to the group in the first place. They will need your support, guidance, and encouragement.

How to Promote Discussion

Discussion is key. The facilitator should avoid lecture formats. Introduce the topic through a short explanation and then begin discussion. One or more direct questions may be necessary to get things going. It is your job to keep it going. Do not allow the discussion to drag or for one person to dominate the conversation.

Good questions that promote discussion include:

- How can you begin to implement what you have learned today? When will you begin?
- Who was in control of that situation?
- What would have been a more productive response?
- Where are you when you feel the most uncomfortable?

You can also begin discussion by first applying the material to yourself and sharing how God is using the material to strengthen you. Then ask others to respond to the material.

Each Group Is Different

No group is the same as any other. Their dynamics are equally unique. People who do not know one another will need time to learn to trust. This chart* shows the three stages of small group development.

	GROUP MEMBERS' THOUGHTS AND FEELINGS	GROUP MEMBERS' ACTIONS
1st STAGE	*Do I belong here? Do they like me? Do I like them?* Anticipation, enthusiasm, anxiety, caution.	Give only basic information about themselves. Accept others on a superficial basis.
2nd STAGE	*Can I trust these people with my thoughts? What is the direction of the group?* Less enthusiasm, more impatience, anxiety.	Some stop attending. Some become vulnerable and begin to assume the goals of the group.
3rd STAGE	*Let's accomplish something together! I like these people.* Acceptance, freedom, vision, determination.	More commitment to goals. Mutual encouragement. Willingness to work through conflict. More leadership is developed.

* Adapted from *Small Group Leader's Handbook*, IVP.

LEADER'S ATTITUDE AND ACTIONS	LEADER'S PLANNED ACTIVITIES
Warmth, enthusiasm, clear communication about the group's direction.	Use "icebreakers" to stimulate interaction. Plan informal time with group leaders. Initiate vulnerability. Use guided discussion instead of lecture.
Empathy, encouragement, flexibility, honesty. Get to know members more intimately. Continue to give clear direction.	More open sharing. Group prayer. Spend time together outside the group. Group involvement in outreach and service.
Encouragement, challenge, clear goals, continued enthusiasm.	Members initiate outreach and service. Members begin to lead others. Training in ministry skills. Quality time together outside the group.

How to Foster Love and Acceptance

Superficial friendliness will not pass for unconditional love. As the group's leader, reflect an attitude of sincerity. This provides a behavior model for others in the group. Make it clear that no one will be criticized or ostracized for their feelings, opinions, or comments. The extent to which you enforce this attitude will be reflected in the level of openness and honesty within the group.

Additionally, outside activities can help strengthen the relationships within the group. You might want to try parties, dinners, games, and retreats. You may also want to call members occasionally, especially those who have missed a meeting.

You may consider pairing people after the group has met about three weeks. These "buddies" can become accountable to one another for following through on homework assignments, maintaining open and honest communication during groups, and working together whenever anxiety strikes.

Meeting Format

Support group meetings typically last one hour to an hour and a half. Decide how long your meetings will last and *stick to the schedule*. Do not go beyond the time you set to end the meeting.

You should come to each meeting prepared to discuss today's topic and to assign next week's homework. Prepare by deciding what *one thing* you hope to accomplish. Then keep the group focused on that single topic. Begin the meeting with prayer. Then stimulate interest in the topic with a 10 minute introduction, including an appropriate Bible reference and a real-life application. This is where you may include other participants by asking that person (ahead of time) to share something about the topic as it applies to his or her life.

Next, ask for discussion. It will be most helpful if you prepare about three open-ended questions and ask for the opinions of several people. Allow discussion and healthy disagreement, but do not permit criticism. Healthy disagreement challenges people to look at things in a new light, but do not let conflicting opinions get out of hand.

Be aware of the needs of each group participant during this time. If someone appears to have a special need, allow the group to focus on that person in a loving, nurturing way. It is up to you to prevent such attention to become condescending or destructive.

Conclude the lesson by asking various participants how they will apply the discussion topic to their lives during the following week. During discussion, do not expect to get an answer from every person in the group. But do not allow one person to always remain silent either. Strike a healthy balance for all participants. Finally, assign next week's assignment and end in prayer.

The dynamics of the group will continue to change. Be flexible, always monitoring the progress of the group and asking for God's leading in determining content.

Be sure to encourage people to share successes each week. This will stimulate enthusiasm and give hope to those who are still struggling.

Getting Help

You can receive small group leadership training from Rapha by calling 1-800-383-HOPE.

APPENDIX C

Support Group Thirteen-Week Outline

The following section is offered as a guide for someone wishing to start a support group using this book as a teaching tool. It is designed around a thirteen-week schedule to give ample time for attenders to understand their anxiety and come to terms with their emotions. The first weeks are intended to gently guide attenders toward recognizing their suppressed feelings. Three weeks should then be dedicated to dealing with feelings (this will produce anxiety in some people—be available for encouragement and support). Final weeks are spent working toward a more positive lifestyle.

Because the dynamics of each group are different, you should remain flexible—without sacrificing the quality of the group experience.

Week 1, Chapter One
   Topic: Understanding anxiety
   Points to cover:
   A. Different kinds of anxiety
   B. Anxiety is caused by a feeling overload with roots
      in past events
   C. Physical symptoms of your anxiety
   D. The need to deal with feelings to overcome anxiety
   Homework: Anxiety inventory

Week 2, Chapter Two
   Topic: The "nature and nurture" equation
   Points to cover:
   A. Heredity and anxiety
   B. Birth order and anxiety
   C. Temperament types
   D. Memories and anxiety
   Homework: Evaluating your first memories

Week 3, Chapter Three
   Topic: Support networks
   Points to cover:
   A. Soul bruises
   B. Values are learned
   C. Four beliefs that trap you
   D. Thoughts and "what ifs"
   E. Attitudes and feelings
   Homework: Evaluating family and peer relationships

Week 4, Chapter Four

Topic: Defense mechanisms
Points to cover:
A. The cancer of unforgiveness
B. Allow considerable group discussion about possible areas of unforgiveness
Homework: Journal personal areas of unforgiveness

Week 5, Chapter Four

Topic: Destructive behavior
Points to cover:
A. Looking for love
B. Life in the fast lane
C. Drowning your sorrows
D. Eating disorders
Homework: Destructive behavior inventory

Week 6, Chapter Five

Topic: Feelings
Points to cover:
A. Consequences of emotional withdrawal
B. Symptoms of suppressed feelings
C. Allow considerable group discussion about physical symptoms of emotional withdrawal
Homework: Journal feelings

Week 7, Chapter Five

Topic: Feelings inventory

Points to cover:

A. How the past teaches us to stuff feelings

B. Feelings and decisions

C. Allow considerable group discussion about past hurts and stuffed feelings

Homework: Journal feelings

Week 8, Chapter Five

Topic: Healing emotional scars

Points to cover:

A. Healthy ways to express feelings

B. Allow considerable group discussion about how to recognize and deal with emotions

Homework: Journal feelings (and continue journaling from now on)

Week 9, Chapter Six

Topic: Belief systems

Points to cover:

A. Discussion about how attenders view God

B. Learning to accept God's love

C. Finding peace

Homework: False belief inventory (question 1 in Looking Inside: Realigning Your Belief System)

Week 10, Chapter Six

Topic: Realigning belief systems
Points to cover:
A. Strengthen your strengths
B. Learning to love yourself
C. Living for God
Homework: Questions 2 through 6 in Looking Inside:
Realigning Your Belief System

Week 11, Chapter Six

Topic: Developing positive self-talk
Points to cover:
A. Consequences of negative self-talk
B. Allow considerable discussion about specific self-
   talk, both positive and negative
Homework: Question 7 in Looking Inside: Realigning
Your Belief System

Week 12, Chapter Seven

Topic: Developing positive relationships
Points to cover:
A. The value of a friend
B. Symptoms of unhealthy relationships
C. Healthy relationships
D. Prayer and friendships
Homework: Plugging the holes in your cup

Week 13, Chapter Eight
Topic: Balanced lifestyle action plan
Points to cover:
A. Let go of the past
B. Understand and respect your phobias
C. Panic plan
D. Living a balanced lifestyle
Homework: Your action plan—and do it!

ANNOTATED BIBLIOGRAPHY

Christian Titles:

Ells, Alfred. *One-Way Relationships: When You Love Them More Than They Love You.* Nashville, TN: Thomas Nelson Publishers, 1990.

This book was written by a counselor who experienced a one-way relationship with his own father. It offers common sense advice on how Christians can develop healthy relationships that bring glory to God.

LaHaye, Beverly. *The Spirit-Controlled Woman.* Eugene, OR: Harvest House Publishers, 1976.

This book sheds light on the idea that temperament type affects your everyday life. It offers ideas on how to deal with life based on your temperament and bring glory to God.

Leman, Kevin. *The Birth Order Book.* Nashville, TN: Thomas Nelson Publishers, 1985.

This book was written by a Christian psychologist. It details the idea that birth order affects a person's view of the world and offers advice on how to overcome the negative aspects of one's outlook.

Leman, Kevin, and Randy Carlson. *Unlocking the Secrets of Your Childhood Memories*. Nashville, TN: Thomas Nelson Publishers, 1989.

Written by two Christian counselors, this book helps readers recall and deal with childhood memories that affect their adult lives. It also offers advice on how to overcome the negative impact of painful memories.

Littauer, Florence. *Personality Plus*. Old Tappan, NJ: Fleming H. Revell Company, 1983.

This book contains a questionnaire that helps the reader determine his or her temperament type and its influence on the person. It offers advice on how to "strengthen the strengths" of each temperament type.

McGee, Robert S. *The Search for Significance*. Houston, TX: Rapha Publishing, 1990, distributed by Word, Inc., Dallas, TX.

This book was written by the President and Founder of Rapha Treatment Centers, a nationally recognized Christian health care organization that provides intensive in-hospital programs from a thoroughy biblical perspective. This book is also available in an expanded version that includes a workbook section to help readers determine how their beliefs developed, the impact of those beliefs today, and how to overcome them.

McGee, Robert S., Jim Craddock, and Pat Springle. *Your Parents and You*. Houston and Dallas, TX: Rapha Publishing/Word, Inc., 1989.

This book details how our parents affect who we are, our outlook on life, and our view of God. It offers a workbook section to help determine and overcome any negative impact of your upbringing.

Minirth, Frank, Paul Meier, and Don Hawkins. *Worry-Free Living.* Nashville, TN: Thomas Nelson Publishers, 1989.

Written by two Christian psychiatrists and a pastor, this book discusses anxiety from a Christian and medical perspective.

Randau, Karen L. *Life Doesn't Have to Hurt.* Nashville, TN: Thomas Nelson Publishers, 1991.

I wrote this book specifically for Christian women. It's a true story about a mother and daughter who overcame the negative effects of alcoholism and abuse in their childhood homes. It offers self-help sections at the end of each chapter to help women understand codependency, sexual abuse, and how to break the cycle of abuse in their lives.

Springle, Pat. *Codependency.* Houston and Dallas, TX: Rapha Publishing/Word, Inc., 1989.

The pain and confusion of codependency are realities for millions of people. This book will help you recognize its painful results in dysfunctional families and, at the same time, offer sound biblical solutions and processes that promise hope and healing.

Wright, H. Norman. *Self-talk, Imagery, and Prayer in Counseling.* Waco, TX: Word, Inc., 1986.

This book was written by a pastor for pastors as part of the Resources for Christian Counseling series.

Secular Titles:

Bass, Ellen, and Laura Davis. *The Courage To Heal: A Guide for Women Survivors of Child Sexual Abuse.* New York, NY: Harper & Row Publishers, Inc., 1988.

This book was written by and for adult survivors of child sexual abuse. I cannot recommend the entire book, but the sections about understanding your emotions and coming to terms with your abuse are excellent.

Beattie, Melody. *Codependent No More.* New York, NY: Harper & Row Publishers, Inc., 1987.

This is one of the secular books that paved the way for a widespread understanding of codependency. It has helped many people recognize the ways they sabotage their own lives.

Bourne, Edmund J., Ph.D. *The Anxiety & Phobia Workbook.* Oakland, CA: New Harbinger Publications, Inc., 1990.

This book offers exercises for understanding and dealing with anxiety. These exercises should be carefully adapted by Christians and replaced with a commitment to pray and meditate on the Scriptures.

BIOGRAPHY

The author, Karen L. Randau, is an adult child of an alcoholic with experience as a lay counselor in a Christian mental health facility. She understands the anguish of anxiety from first-hand experience. Her career as an author began at an early age—as soon as she learned to read and write. Now, as then, her writings represent a time to dig deep within herself . . . a time to journal feelings and desires common to most of us.